THINKING
LIKE A
CHRISTIAN

THINKING
LIKE A
CHRISTIAN

*Understanding and Living
a Biblical Worldview*

DAVID NOEBEL AND CHUCK EDWARDS

BROADMAN
&HOLMAN
PUBLISHERS

Nashville, Tennessee

Copyright © 2002 by David Noebel and Chuck Edwards

Published in 2002 by Broadman & Holman Publishers
Nashville, Tennessee

DEWEY: 248.48
SUBHD: CHRISTIAN LIFE / DISCIPLESHIP

Cover and interior design by
The Gregory Group and Paul T. Gant, Art & Design—Nashville, TN

ISBN 0-8054-3896-3

4 5   06 05 04

TABLE OF CONTENTS

BY JOSH MCDOWELL

Speaker, and author of best-sellers
Right from Wrong, Why Wait?, and
Evidence That Demands a Verdict

This generation is faced with the greatest and most serious cultural crisis in history. And the crisis is a direct result of a radical change in the way people view what is true.

I've given more than 23,000 talks to students in universities and high schools in 100 countries around the world. What I'm finding is this: When I make a statement about the deity of Christ, the resurrection, or the reliability of Scripture, I have people come up to me and say, "What right do you have to say that? You're being intolerant! What right do you have to judge anyone's moral life?"

These questions come from a totally different view of life than was once the case. We are now living in not just a post-Christian culture, but an anti-Christian culture!

That's why you face a challenge unlike any other in recent history. Before you can know how to respond to our changing culture, you must first understand how the Bible relates to all of life.

In the pages of this journal, you will encounter a biblical worldview. Each daily session will be an eye-opening experience that gives hope, meaning and a greater understanding of how God fits into every part of your life.

I challenge you to spend time in this journal each day. Then, like the leaders from the small tribe of Issachar in the Old Testament, you will understand the times and know what you should do (1 Chronicles 12:32).

Josh

ABOUT THIS STUDY

This journal is designed to help you develop a biblical worldview. Its major topics of focus are taken from our book Thinking Like a Christian. *When this book is cited, it will be set apart with the notation "(TLAC, ___)," to indicate the page from which the quote is taken.*

Since the Bible is the source of the only thoroughly accurate worldview, you also will find numerous Scripture quotations. We've included them either in the side margins or at the end of the chapter to make sure you can get to them easily. So please read each one carefully. They're taken from a fresh, new Bible translation–the Holman Christian Standard Bible®*–translated into English from the original biblical languages.*

You may be using this journal as a course for individual home study, to enhance a weekly Bible study in church, or on campus. Whichever way, you may want to have a copy of Thinking Like a Christian *for a more in-depth study of the biblical Christian worldview.*

May God speed you on this mind-expanding journey!

Yours along the way,

David A. Noebel, President
Chuck Edwards, Director of Bible Study Curriculum
Summit Ministries
Manitou Springs, Colorado

WEEK 1: INTRODUCTION

DISCOVER A WHOLE NEW WORLD

You are about to begin a journey into another world, but not the world travel kind of journey. These pages will take you into the world of the mind—the world of ideas.

On this journey you will be challenged to compare your ideas about life, and the ideas presented by our culture, with ideas that come from the Bible. Through the process, you will be developing what is called a "biblical worldview."

THE MAIN POINT: A worldview is a way of understanding the world and your place in it.

A MAP FOR THE JOURNEY

As this journal becomes part of your daily routine, you will begin to see the big picture of how the Bible relates to every area of life. The eleven-week study is divided into the following topics:

Week 1   Introduction: How the Bible relates to every area of life!

Week 2   Theology: Is there a God, and what is God like?

Week 3   Philosophy: What's real, and how do I know what's true?

Week 4   Biology: How did life originate, and what difference does it make?

Week 5   Psychology: What is man's basic nature?

Week 6   Ethics: How do I know what's right and wrong?

Week 7   Sociology: What are the foundational institutions for society?

Week 8   Law: What laws rule our lives and why?

Week 9   Politics: What is the best type of government?

Week 10   Economics: What are the principles for making and spending money?

Week 11   History: What can I learn from the past, and where is history headed?

WEEK 1, DAY 1

REMOVING THE MENTAL BLINDERS

THE BLINDERS PHENOMENON

When wearing blinders—you know, the things that a mule or horse wears on either side of its eyes—the poor animal can only see what is directly in front of it. It knows nothing about the rest of the world, only what is at its feet.

Unfortunately, many Christians also experience what might be called the "blinders phenomenon." Christian philosopher and author Francis Schaeffer describes it this way:

> *The basic problem of the Christians in this country in the last eighty years or so, in regard to society and in regard to government, is that they have seen things in bits and pieces instead of totals* (TLAC, 8).

What does Schaeffer mean by seeing things in "bits and pieces instead of totals"?

_____

_____

Seeing bits and pieces is like going through life wearing mental blinders. We see a certain idea or cultural issue with a limited focus, oblivious to how it relates to the larger issues of life.

What has been the result of Christians having this "bits and pieces" focus? List some of the specific cultural changes our society has experienced in the last eighty years.

_____

_____

For the most part, are these positive or negative changes?

    ❏   Positive   ❏   Negative

Francis Schaeffer blames America's drift toward secularism and injustice on the Christian community's failure to apply its worldview to every facet of society.

Do you agree or disagree with Schaeffer's assessment? How might Christians have been withdrawing from the areas of education, government, and social services?

_____

_____

Jesus said that His followers should be like salt and light to their culture (see Matthew 5:13). In thinking about your response to Schaeffer's view, consider what biblical principles would help you evaluate the role Christians ought to play in society?

_____

Schaeffer also argues that our problem is related to the lack of a total world and lifeview. If the problem is a misunderstanding of how a biblical worldview can matter to society, we must get a handle on exactly what that worldview is.

"WORLDVIEW" DEFINED

A worldview offers a particular perspective on everything. This study focuses on ten disciplines which influence all of life: theology, philosophy, ethics, biology, psychology, sociology, law, politics, economics, and history. Once you understand how your worldview affects your understanding of these areas, you will find ways to apply it to still other aspects of culture, such as the arts.

What do you think: Does the Bible have something to say about each of those ten disciplines?

     ❑ Yes!

     ❑ Maybe, convince me.

     ❑ Definitely not!

An even more important question is this: Can you defend a biblical view of each discipline?

     ❑ Yes! All ten.

     ❑ Most, but not all.

     ❑ Maybe a few.

     ❑ Sorry, ask me again at the end of the book.

Matthew 5:13

You are the salt of the earth. But if the salt should lose its taste, how can it be made salty? It's no longer good for anything but to be thrown out and trampled on by men.

Over the next several weeks, you will have an eye-opening experience as we discuss each of ten disciplines in light of principles found in the Bible! This process should lead you away from a bits and pieces view of life to an understanding of the larger picture—a total, biblical worldview.

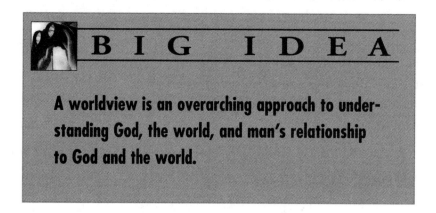

BIG IDEA

A worldview is an overarching approach to understanding God, the world, and man's relationship to God and the world.

This week's key verses are Colossians 2:6-7. As you read them, think about how you should live in Christ.

WEEK 1 KEY VERSES

> Colossians 2:6-7 *Therefore as you have received Christ Jesus the Lord, walk in Him, [7]rooted and built up in Him and established in the faith, just as you were taught, and overflowing with thankfulness.*

 PRAY ABOUT IT!

Write a prayer asking God to remove any mental blinders that are keeping you from seeing the world through biblical eyes.

_____

_____

_____

_____

DAY 1 SUMMARY

A worldview is an _____ approach to understanding _____, the _____, and man's _____ to God and the world.

WEEK 1, DAY 2
THINKING LIKE A CHRISTIAN

THINKING ABOUT THINKING

Let's face it. Thinking can be hard work! It's much easier to watch a movie or just relax to the music of your favorite CD.

But the movies you watch and the music you listen to are filled with ideas about life. Whether you recognize it or not, they influence the way you think. And if they're going to shape your life, it's important to understand exactly what these ideas are.

As you continue through this journal you will see that thinking has its own rewards—rewards which are more meaningful than a popular movie and longer lasting than the latest hit CD.

THINKING LIKE A CHRISTIAN

Being a Christian is more than just doing "religious" things like devotional Bible reading, praying and staying away from sinful habits. It should affect the very way we think about life.

Jesus describes the importance of using your mind when it comes to being His disciple. In **Matthew 22:37-38**, He says:

> *"You shall love the Lord your God with all your heart, with all your soul, and with all your mind." This is the greatest and most important commandment.*

Notice: You are to love God not only with your heart and soul, but also with all your _____!

What does it mean to love God with your mind?

_____

In addition to loving God with all your mind, there is another biblical principle Christians should follow. In **Romans 12:2**, Paul writes:

> *Do not be conformed to this age, but be transformed by the renewing of your mind, so that you may discern what is the good, pleasing, and perfect will of God.*

Here, Paul talks about knowing God's will for your life. He says that you come to know God's will by the _____ _____ _____ _____.

YOUR MIND MATTERS

Jesus said that your mind is involved in loving God, and Paul emphasizes that you must renew your mind in order to know God's will. In light of these two principles, how important is it to think like a Christian in each worldview category? (Circle your answer.)

Not Important			Somewhat Important				Very Important		
1	2	3	4	5	6	7	8	9	10

Your mind really does matter. Being a Christian is much more than just a personal, private relationship with God. It influences every aspect of your life and how you relate to others. That is the nature of a total worldview.

 ## PUTTING ON YOUR THINKING CAP

All right. So, let's think like Christians! Look in a newspaper and scan the front-page headlines.

If you are a part of a group study:

> Pick an article from a newspaper or magazine that you find interesting. Think about the big idea of the article. Does it fit into one of the ten worldview categories? Which one? Write the category at the top of the article, and bring it to the next group meeting to share with your friends.

If you are involved in individual home-based learning:

> Select five articles from newspapers or magazines that you find interesting. Think about the big idea of each article. Does it fit into one of the ten worldview categories? Which one? Write the category at the top of each article. Discuss the articles with your teaching parent.

 ## PRAY ABOUT YOUR MIND

Take a minute to thank God for the wonderful mind He has given you. Ask Him to expand your understanding of the Bible's view of life, your life, and how you fit into His world.

WEEK 1, DAY 3
IS IT SECULAR, OR IS IT SACRED?

MIND YOUR OWN BUSINESS!

Many people believe that when Christians. . . attempt to speak to such "secular" disciplines as politics, economics, biology, and law, they are overstepping their bounds. "Mind your own business," we are told. . . . In short, isn't there a difference between the secular and the sacred? (TLAC, 10)

In starting this journey into the world of ideas, maybe you've been asking the same questions: Shouldn't we Christians mind our own business? Why waste time on worldly issues?

SECULAR VS. SACRED

"Sacred" means: Areas in life that relate to religion and religious principles.

Is a Christian's life divided into two different areas—the worldly, or secular, and the religious, or sacred? What do you think?

- ❒   Yes, some areas of life are secular and others are sacred.

- ❒   No, there is no difference between the two; everything is secular.

- ❒   No, there is no difference between the two; everything is sacred.

- ❒   I'm not sure; convince me!

Give reasons for your answer:

_____

_____

THINKING ABOUT REALITY

To evaluate this issue about the secular and the sacred, read the following quote from Dietrich Bonhoeffer, a respected German theologian who spoke out against the Nazis during World War II:

There are not two realities, but only one reality, and that is the reality of God, which has become manifest in Christ in the reality of the world (TLAC, 10).

▼ How many realities are there? _____

▼ What is that one reality? _____

If God created the world as one reality, wouldn't it make sense that we should think about everything in the world the way God does?

From the biblical Christian perspective, the ten disciplines addressed in this study reflect various attributes of God and His creative order. God created mankind with theological, philosophical, ethical, biological, psychological, sociological, legal, political, economic, and historical dimensions. We live within all of these categories. Why? Because that's the way God created us.

GOD'S CREATIVE ORDER

In the following passages, look at each example of God's creation. Reflect on the Bible verses noted below, and the ten worldview disciplines to fill in the missing words (theology, philosophy, ethics, biology, psychology, sociology, law, politics, economics, history).

Genesis 1:1 "In the beginning God created the heavens and the earth" is value-laden with ramifications for _____ and philosophy.

Genesis 2:9 "the knowledge of good and evil" contains ramifications for _____.

Genesis 1:21 "according to their kinds" _____.

Genesis 2:7 "the man became a living being" _____.

Genesis 1:28 "Be fruitful and multiply, fill the earth" _____ and ecology.

Genesis 3:11 "I had forbidden you" _____.

Genesis 9:6 "Whoever sheds man's blood, by man his blood will be shed"
Politics and _____.

Genesis 1:29 "This will be food for you" _____.

Genesis 10:1 "These are the family records of Noah's sons: Shem, Ham and Japheth . . ." _____.

All ten worldview categories are addressed in the opening book of the Bible because they manifest and accent certain aspects of God's creative order. God designed the world to operate within these distinct areas.

NOW WHAT DO YOU THINK?

So, which is it: Is life secular or sacred? Based on what we've said so far, fill in the following sentence:

After careful consideration of the Scriptures, I believe all of life is _____.

 ## THINKING AND PRAYING

1) Think about an area in your life that you are keeping in a "secular" box. What comes to mind? _____

2) What is God's view on that issue? _____

3) Write a prayer about your commitment to live according to God's worldview:

_____

_____

_____

DAY 3 SUMMARY

Why is it that everything is "sacred"?

_____

_____

REVIEW KEY VERSES

Colossians 2:6-7 *Therefore as you have received Christ Jesus the Lord, walk in Him,* [7] _____ *and* _____ *in Him and established in the faith, just as you were taught, and overflowing with thankfulness.*

WEEK 1, DAY 4

WESTERN CIVILIZATION AND THE BIBLE

ATHLETIC SHOES AND WORLDVIEWS

Why do people in the United States wear Nikes? (No, it's not because they look cool or they make you run faster and jump higher.)

Or why do you wear expensive sports shoes instead of walking around barefoot? (No, it's not about comfort.)

Actually, the issue is: Why do we even have all the different options of shoes to wear, instead of bare shelves staring us in the face?

Don't have a clue? Maybe it's because you usually don't think about things in that way. When you do, you're actually thinking in terms of a worldview.

You see, most people living in India or the jungles of South America do not wear expensive athletic shoes. Know why? It's not so much a matter of economics as it is their worldview. Read on to find out why.

WESTERN CIVILIZATION 101

The culture of Western Europe and North America is called "western civilization." Western culture grew out of a Greek and, ultimately, a biblical point of view. As a result of the biblical mindset of early modern scientists (Galileo, Newton, etc.), modern science flourished. This in turn led to modern technology, a free-market economy, greater prosperity for more people, and—you guessed it—Nikes!

And it all started with a certain way of looking at life—a worldview based not on Buddhism, not on Hinduism, not on paganism, not on humanism . . . but on the Bible.

This does not mean that a biblical worldview only relates to people in Europe and North America, of course. The point is that biblical Christianity is true for everybody everywhere because it describes the real world. And since it is true, it relates to all of life.

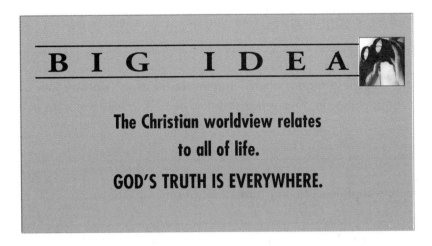

BIG IDEA

The Christian worldview relates
to all of life.

GOD'S TRUTH IS EVERYWHERE.

You can find the truth of Christianity wherever you look. For example, George Gilder is not only an outstanding economic philosopher but also a sociologist who became a Christian while seeking sociological truth.

"Christianity is true," says George Gilder, "and its truth will be discovered anywhere you look very far." (TLAC, 7)

List some of the "anywhere's" that a person might look to discover the truth of Christianity:

_____

_____

Did your list include any of the ten categories that make up a worldview? If not, should you add those categories to your list? (Hint: "Yes" would be a good answer!)

THE HEART OF A BIBLICAL WORLDVIEW

The center of a biblical worldview is found in the following verses from **Colossians 2:6, 8**:

⁶Therefore as you have received Christ Jesus the Lord, walk in Him, . . . ⁸Be careful that no one takes you captive through philosophy and empty deceit based on human tradition, based on the elemental forces of the world, and not based on Christ.

These verses say that you should beware of philosophy and _____ based on _____ tradition.

What does Paul mean by "empty deceit"? (Note: you might do a word study on those two terms.)

_____

Can you think of any current examples where "human tradition" is contrary to a Christian world-view? (Hint: think about common slogans heard today, like "If it feels good, do it.")

_____

_____

In what ways can deceitful philosophies or human traditions capture you?

_____

_____

A biblical worldview is founded on Jesus Christ. On your journey into the world of ideas, you will discover how Jesus is the center of every aspect of life. He affects everything about your life and everything you do.

If you are wearing Nikes today (or any other brand of athletic shoe), you can literally thank Jesus for it! Apart from Him, we might be going barefoot!

 PRAY ABOUT IT!

Ask God to allow you to see the world through Jesus' eyes.

DAY 4 SUMMARY

Where can you look to discover the truth of Christianity?

_____

_____

DIGGING DEEPER: *For more information about how a biblical worldview led to modern science, see chapter 1 of* The Soul of Science: Christian Faith and Natural Philosophy, *by Nancy Pearcey and Charles Thaxton, or study the lives of the early modern scientists such as Kepler, Newton, Cuvier, Faraday, Morse, or Pasteur. We will also return to this during our study of Biology, Week 4, Days 1 and 2. Online resources on this topic are available at:*

www.leaderu.com/offices/schaefer/docs/scientists.html and www.lcr.org/pubs/imp/imp-103.htm

WEEK 1, DAY 5

THE FOUNDATION OF A BIBLICAL WORLDVIEW

WHY THE LEANING TOWER IS LEANING

What's the most important part of a building?

While there are many parts that make up a building—floors, walls, roof, windows, doors—any builder will tell you that the most important part is the foundation. If the foundation is not laid correctly, the entire building could topple.

So, why is the Leaning Tower of Pisa leaning? Because its foundation was not laid correctly.

As with constructing a building, it's important to lay a solid foundation for your worldview.

LAYING THE RIGHT FOUNDATION

What would you say is the foundation for a biblical Christian worldview?

_____

Some people would say that the Bible is the foundation. But the Bible is simply the way that God has chosen to communicate His truth to us. It is not the foundation itself.

Someone else might choose faith as the foundation. But faith is our response to God's truth. It is not the foundation itself.

Others say that God is the foundation. This is getting closer, but **Colossians 1:15** is more specific:

> He [Jesus Christ] is the image of the invisible God, the firstborn over all creation.

This verse tells us that Jesus is God made visible to us. We can get a picture of God by looking at Jesus. And Jesus is the "most important thing" over the entire created universe.

THE SOLID ROCK

Look at the rest of that passage in Colossians 1 to find other reasons that Jesus is the starting point of a biblical worldview:

[17] He is before all things, and by Him all things hold together. [18] He is also the head of the body, the church; He is the beginning, the firstborn from the dead, so that He might come to have first place in everything. [19] Because all the fullness was pleased to dwell in Him, [20] and to reconcile everything to Himself through Him by making peace through the blood of His cross—whether things on earth or things in heaven.

Jesus   . . . _____ all things together.

        . . . is the _____ of the church.

        . . . has _____ over everything else, including death.

        . . . is the _____ of God.

        . . . _____ everything to himself through his _____.

Do you get the idea that Jesus is the most important thing in the entire universe? This passage indicates that He is the solid foundation for developing a correct worldview.

JESUS, THE FOUNDATION

When Christ told the woman who spoke of the Messiah, "I am He, the One speaking to you" (John 4:26), He was telling her the most fundamental truth of all. What Christ said concerning life and death, the saved and lost condition of mankind, body and soul, and truth encompasses the central precepts of the Christian worldview. Christ is its cornerstone. He is the way, the truth, and the life (John 14:6) (TLAC, 15).

Taking Christ out of culture causes society to fall apart, too. Do you see any evidences that our society is falling apart? What are they?

_____

_____

BUT DOES THIS MEAN. . .?

▼ You can't separate religious ideas from government policy?   Yes / No

▼ Science begins with assuming a Creator, namely, Jesus Christ?   Yes / No

▼ There are absolute moral standards such as saving sexual intimacy for marriage?   Yes / No

▼ I should speak up and share with others reasons why Jesus is the beginning point for all knowledge?   Yes / No

If you answered YES to all of the above questions, you are well on your way to "understanding the times" from a biblical point of view.

SOMETHING TO THINK ABOUT—AND PRAY ABOUT

Review today's lesson and pick the one or two ideas that intrigue you most—maybe that Jesus is the cornerstone of your worldview, or maybe a personal application about speaking up for the truth in your community. You decide, and write a prayer or praise about it.

_____

_____

DAY 5 SUMMARY

Write the key idea about Jesus from today's study:

_____

_____

WEEK 1 SUMMARY

Life is like a gigantic jigsaw puzzle. When we assemble the pieces, a clear picture comes together. God designed the picture so that everything in it relates to Him, down to the smallest piece of the puzzle. The Bible paints the total picture for us, and Jesus Christ is the foundation of the picture. We call this picture a biblical Christian worldview.

REVIEW KEY VERSES

Colossians 2:6-7 *Therefore as you have received Christ Jesus the Lord, walk in Him,* *⁷rooted and built up in Him and _____ in the faith, just as you were _____,* *and overflowing with thankfulness.*

NOTE: If you are involved in a group study on worldviews, be sure to bring an article from the newspaper and your Bible to the next group meeting.

If you're doing an individual study, use a folder to keep your articles together for ready reference.

N O T E S

WEEK 2: THEOLOGY

A CLOSE ENCOUNTER OF THE GOD KIND

Making sense out of our world is a pretty big task. Sometimes, you may feel confused and a little overwhelmed in trying to understand why people act in certain ways and why things happen the way they do. Having a well-thought-out worldview, though, helps the pieces make sense.

Putting together a worldview is much like working a puzzle—you start by finding the pieces that fit around the edge. The pieces that frame in any worldview answer the question: "What about God?" When we ask that question, we are dealing with the subject of "theology."

Theology is the study of the existence, nature, and attributes of God. Or, to put it another way, theology answers the following key questions: "Is there a God?" and "What is God like?"

This week you will look into both questions. In the process, you will:

▼ Encounter what it's like to have pizza with an atheist

▼ Make the connection between watches, minds, morals and God

▼ Learn that God has a special message for you

▼ Discover how God has personalized that communication in the person of Jesus Christ

To start looking for those outside pieces of your worldview, read on!

WEEK 2, DAY 1
GOD'S SPOKESMAN

LUNCH WITH AN ATHEIST

One Saturday, you're out for pizza with a group of friends and find that one of the gang has brought along someone you don't know. Being the charming, outgoing person you are, you strike up a conversation with the new guy, Skip.

As you're chowing down your pizza supreme, Skip tells you that his parents sued the last school he attended because the coach had a prayer before the football games. He shows you his membership card with the American Atheist Association. You take a bite of pepperoni, cheese and olives and weakly mumble that you attend the church where that coach is a member.

Skip then asks you a question that makes you choke on the crust and leaves a string of mozzarella cheese dangling from your mouth: "So, you're a Christian. Tell me, how do you know there is a god?" At that precise moment, the entire restaurant grows strangely silent, and every person in the room turns and looks at you!

NOW . . . What do you do?

You may wish you could drop to your knees and pray that God would answer Skip with a voice from heaven. Or that you could at least whip out your cell phone, call your pastor and let him talk to Skip. But Skip's question can lead you—and him!—to some real answers about God.

What he's really asking is "How do you know God is real?" And to that, God Himself has some very convincing answers.

ASK THE HEAVENS!

God has not left us to figure out by ourselves if He is real. Do you know how God has communicated to people everywhere, even those who can't read?

THE *REAL* COMMUNICATIONS NETWORK

Take a look at **Psalm 19:1-4** and answer the following questions:

1)   Verse 1—What role does the physical universe play?

_____

BIG IDEA

General revelation is God's communication
of Himself to all persons,
at all times, and in all places.

Psalm 19:1-4

*"The heavens declare the
glory of God; the skies
proclaim the work of his
hands.
²Day after day they pour
forth speech; night after
night they display
knowledge.
³There is no speech or
language where their
voice is not heard.
⁴Their voice goes out
into all the earth, their
words to the ends of the
world. In the heavens he
has pitched a tent for
the sun . . . "*

What does this imply? This revelation from God allows all
_____ everywhere, at any _____, and in every _____
to understand that God is! He exists! He is real!

2)   Verse 2—What two things does nature pour forth and
display?

_____

_____

3)   Verses 3-4—Is this knowledge of God communicated to
people everywhere?
  ❑ Yes
  ❑ No

4)   In what way is it communicated?

_____

_____

Every person on planet Earth can hear and understand what
nature is saying. In a big, loud voice, it screams out, "God Is!"
*Skip may not care to admit it, but the universe itself suggests that
there is a God.*

SPEAKING OUT FOR GOD

Because nature speaks so plainly, the apostle Paul speaks out boldly and says there is no excuse for anyone not to believe in God.   Look at **Romans 1:20**:

> *From the creation of the world His invisible attributes, that is, His eternal power and divine nature, have been clearly seen, being understood through what He has made. As a result, people are without excuse.*

This is why everywhere you go on our planet, you find cultures that believe in a Supreme Being. Nature has told them that God exists. So, from the verse in Romans:

How long has God been made known? _____

What has He made known? _____

In what ways do you think the universe displays God's "eternal power"?

_____

_____

God's "divine nature" is shown in what ways?

_____

_____

Paul concludes that no one anywhere at any time has an excuse for not knowing that GOD IS!

YOU ARE GOD'S SPOKESPERSON

Think of someone you know who may not be paying attention to God's communication through the natural world. Ask God to use you as His "spokesperson" to that individual. Write the name of the person you are praying for: _____

DAY 1 SUMMARY

God's communication about Himself through nature is known as g_____ r_____.

Tell in your own words what that means: _____

_____

WEEK 2 KEY VERSE

Colossians 2:9 *For in Him the entire fullness of God's nature dwells bodily.*

WEEK 2, DAY 2
WATCHES, MINDS, AND MORALS

A REVEALING RIDDLE

What do watches, minds, and morals have in common?
(Take sixty seconds to think about your answer and write it below)

_____

_____

There may be many creative ways you could solve the riddle, but as with most riddles, there is a "right" answer: Each of the three things can be used to point to the reality of God. Once you think through the questions below, you'll be ready to explain that to someone like Skip!

Write out your ideas to the following questions or statements:

1) How does a watch illustrate the reality of a God?

_____

_____

2) Our minds point to the reality of God because

_____

_____

3) The fact that we have ideas of right and wrong (we call them 'morals') demonstrates the reality of God because

_____

_____

Each piece of the riddle represents a very important point about God's existence. Check out the following three statements and compare them with the answers you wrote above.

(1) WE LIVE IN A DESIGNED UNIVERSE

Anglican clergyman William Paley argued in Natural Theology . . . *that a man chancing upon a watch in the wilderness could not conclude that the watch had simply always existed; rather, the obvious design of the watch—not only its internal makeup but also the fact that it clearly exists for a purpose—would necessarily imply the existence of its designer. Paley went on to substitute the universe for the watch and contended that a mechanism so obviously designed as the universe necessitated the existence of a grand*

Designer. (TLAC, 24-5)

According to Paley, if a watch implies a "watchmaker," then a designed universe implies a

_____.

And guess what? A "Designer" capable of designing the entire universe would have to be "God." This "Designer/Creator/God" is not just a religious concept. The idea of a "Creator" is the most scientific conclusion you can reach based on observations of the real world. Why is this true?

_____

_____

(2) WE LIVE IN AN INTELLIGENT UNIVERSE

Still another twist on the argument for the general revelation of God's existence is presented by C. S. Lewis. "Suppose there were no intelligence behind the universe," says Lewis. "In that case nobody designed my brain for the purpose of thinking. Thought is merely the by-product of some atoms within my skull. But if so, how can I trust my own thinking to be true?" asks Lewis (TLAC, 25)

Think about "thinking" for a moment. The very fact that you are "thinking" raises an important question: Where do your thoughts come from? (Pick the answer you think is best.)

❏ Electrical impulses between the synapses of the cells in my brain.

❏ I try not to think—it gives me a headache.

❏ A mental/spiritual source.

❏ It somehow just happens.

Your mind is more that just the chemical processes of some "gray matter." Since there is apparently more to our minds than just our physical brains, there must be a God who created our ability to think.

Therefore, minds imply a Divine I_____.

(3) WE LIVE IN A MORAL UNIVERSE

There is a third line of thinking that directs us to the conclusion that God is real.

C. E. M. Joad, who was an atheist for much of his professional career, wrote a book entitled The Recovery of Belief *shortly before his death. This book traces his gradual*

advance toward God and Jesus Christ. Joad was largely convinced by his observation of human nature that a moral law exists and that men often flaunt that law. (TLAC, 25)

What reason led this atheist to be convinced that God is real?

_____

If there is no God, then the only foundation for morals is a universe of molecules and energy. An impersonal universe is not a very promising source for ideas like "love one another" or "do not murder."

CONSIDER THIS!
MORALS IMPLY A MORAL *LAW-GIVER.*

If naturalism were true, then saying that certain human actions are "bad" would make just as much sense as saying that a leaf blowing in the wind was "bad." How often have you done that?

But since we do have these ideas like "love is good" and "murder is evil," there must be a moral, spiritual dimension from which these moral ideals flow. This moral source is God.

Therefore, morals imply a moral L_____-g_____

PRAYING PRAISES

Read **Psalm 8** (see sidebar). In these nine verses the writer is praising God for the works of His hands, the natural universe. Think about these verses, and turn the thoughts of the psalmist into your own words of praise.

_____

_____

_____

DAY 2 SUMMARY

What are the three ways that general revelation tells us that God exists?

_____

Psalm 8

O Lord, our Lord, how magnificent is Your name throughout the earth! You have covered the heavens with Your splendor.

²Because of Your adversaries, You have set up a fortification from the mouths of children and nursing infants, to silence the enemy and the avenger.

³When I observe Your heavens, the work of Your fingers, the moon and the stars that You set in place,

⁴What is man, that You remember him, the son of man, that You look after him?

⁵You made him little less than God, and crowned him with glory and honor.

⁶You made him lord over the works of Your hands; You put everything under his feet:

⁷All the sheep and oxen, as well as animals in the wild,

⁸Birds of the sky, and fish of the sea passing through the currents of the seas.

⁹O Lord, our Lord, how magnificent is Your name throughout all the earth!

WEEK 2, DAY 3
GOD'S THREE R's MAKE CONNECTIONS

Yesterday, we looked at how the moral universe points to a God who is holy. Because His holiness is so significant, this idea of how He built morals into the universe is worth exploring a little further. It's an important way He connects with us in life.

THE GOD CONNECTION

There are at least three over-arching characteristics of God:

> God is . . . ruler
>
> . . . righteous
>
> . . . relational

Which of the three "R's" relates to God's moral character?

> "God is R_____."

Look at the verses below and see how God's righteousness is reflected in His dealings with mankind:

> **Psalm 7:9** *Let the evil of the wicked come to an end, but establish the righteous. The One who examines the thoughts and emotions **is a righteous God.***
>
> **Psalm 11:7** *For the LORD is righteous; He loves righteous deeds. The upright will see His face.*

Summarize these verses in your own words:

_____

_____

There is another side to God's righteousness. Read the following verses as you think through what is said about living a moral life:

> **Psalm 119:7-9** *I will praise You with a sincere heart when I learn Your righteous judgments. ⁸I will keep Your statutes; never abandon me. ⁹How can a young man keep his way pure? By keeping Your word.*

How do God's righteous laws help us know how to live?

_____

_____

THE WORLDVIEW CONNECTION

The sentence below is based on a summary of Joad's reasoning from human nature to God. (Draw a line from each phrase to the worldview category that describes that concept.)

C. E. M. Joad was a seeker of truth. . .	Theology
who *was studying human nature. . .*	Philosophy
and *came to realize that men were moral creatures. . . .*	Ethics
which *led to his conclusion that there must be a God . . .*	Psychology

Do you see the connection between these different parts of a worldview? Someone can be seeking truth (philosophy) by studying human nature (psychology) and make observations about morality (ethics) that lead to conclusions about the existence and nature of God (theology).

It all fits together to form a total view of reality. The Bible presents a coherent way of understanding ourselves and the world around us.

 ## THE LIFE CONNECTION

Not only is God perfectly righteous in all His ways, but He distinguishes between good and evil in our behavior. Notice how important this is in **Proverbs 5:21-23**:

> *For a man's ways are before the LORD's eyes, and He considers all his paths. ²² A wicked man's iniquities entrap him; he is entangled in the ropes of his own sin. ²³ When there is no instruction, he will die and be lost through his great stupidity.*

Describe in your own words the principle from these verses and how you can apply that principle to your life situation.

The principle:_____

The application:_____

DAY 3 SUMMARY

What does God's righteousness imply for your life?

_____

WEEK 2 KEY VERSE

Colossians 2:9 *For in Him the entire fullness of God's nature dwells bodily.*

WEEK 2, DAY 4
GOD HAS SOMETHING SPECIAL FOR YOU

WHO'S TO SAY WHAT GOD IS LIKE?

You have a new neighbor, Shirley. After visiting your church, she informs you that her view of God is quite different than yours. In fact, she believes God is an impersonal cosmic energy that permeates everything in the entire universe.

You share with her how the universe displays the glory of God. Shirley agrees, but goes on to say that everything in the universe—the rocks, the trees, dolphins, the asteroids, the stars, human life—is a part of the cosmic energy that, blended together, comprise "god."

What would you say next to help Shirley understand that God is not an impersonal force, but a personal Being? (Hint: check your notes from Day 2.)

_____

_____

So, you explain that humans have a mind, and this points to a personal God. Way to go! But then she says that our minds are just a part of the impersonal "cosmic consciousness" called "god." (Rats! where does she keep coming up with this stuff?)

What other line of evidence could you use to help her understand that God is real? (Don't forget about yesterday's study!)

_____

_____

Well, after you comment that within the heart of every person is a moral sense of right and wrong, and that this means God is moral, you find she actually agrees with you—sort of. She agrees that we must do what is good because otherwise we will be reincarnated as an inferior animal to work off our bad karma.

Karma! What's karma? You decide to drop the subject and tell Shirley you have to rush home and check email!

WE'VE GOT A PROBLEM HERE

It seems that the universe is not too precise about the exact nature of God. Oh, sure, nature proclaims there is a God, but someone of a different religion can appeal to nature and arrive at a conclusion about God that is very different from yours.

The last two days we looked at what can be known about God through general revelation, or the created order. But the question is: What characteristics of God can be gleaned from the natural world? As you think about that question, put a check by the qualities below that you think can be known from observing creation:

_____ God is real   _____ God judges sin

_____ God is Creator   _____ God sent Jesus to die for man's sin

_____ God is intelligent   _____ God is in control of everything

_____ God is holy   _____ God is love

While the universe proclaims that God is real, Creator, intelligent and holy, it is silent on what God is like beyond the attributes of power, intelligence and morality. The four qualities in the second column are not revealed to us through nature. The ideas of God's love, judgment, salvation, and sovereignty are not understood by observing the world around us. We must find out about these attributes in another way.

The problem with general revelation is just that. . . it's too *general!* As we observed, a cosmic humanist like Shirley can appeal to nature to describe her idea of god just as you used nature to defend your view.

But God has not left us to muddle through life with just a vague, general picture of Him. He has taken other steps to reveal to us a clear image of who He is and what He is like.

SPECIAL REVELATION TO THE RESCUE

> *On the one hand, general revelation is God's communication of Himself to all persons, at all times, and in all places. Special revelation, on the other hand, involves God's particular communications and manifestations which are available now only by consultation of certain sacred writings.* (TLAC, 21)

Use the following questions to dig deeper into the description of special revelation by looking at each part of it:

What does "God's particular communications" mean? For example, can you think of any of the many ways that God communicated to people in the *past* which are recorded in the Bible?

_____

_____

_____

What does "manifestations" mean, and how are they different from God's "communications"?

_____

_____

How have God's past communications and manifestations been preserved for us?

_____

_____

Special revelation means that God takes the initiative to communicate to mankind (that's the "revelation" part) through specific and particular ways (that's the "special" part). In the past, God revealed Himself in a number of different ways: dreams, direct thoughts, direct encounters—even a burning bush! The human authors of the Bible wrote down what God communicated to them so that we can read about it today.

What's so special about special revelation? It's specific! It gets down to the details about who God is and His plan for mankind.

SPECIAL REVELATION EXPLAINS GOD

The Bible is emphatic in describing God as a person who is aware of Himself. In **Isaiah 44:6**, God says, *"I am the first and I am the last, and there is no God besides me."* In **Exodus 3:14**, God says to Moses, *"I Am Who I Am."*

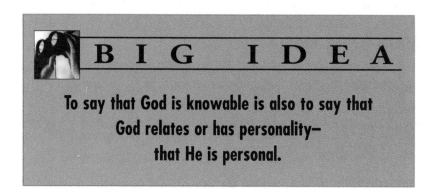

BIG IDEA

To say that God is knowable is also to say that God relates or has personality— that He is personal.

God's self-awareness, His emotions, and His self-determining will make up the core of His divine personality.

Remember the three over-arching characteristics of God:

God is . . . ruler

. . . righteous

. . . relational

Which of the three "R's" corresponds to God's desire to be intimately acquainted with His creatures?

God is R_____.

RELATING TO A PERSONAL GOD

As you pray today, reflect on the fact that God is a personal Being who desires to have a personal relationship with you.

DAY 4 SUMMARY

To say that God is knowable is also to say that God "_____" or has personality—that He is "_____."

What makes special revelation so important to our understanding of God?

_____

_____

DIGGING DEEPER: *Many skeptics of Christianity point out that the Bible is not a trustworthy revelation of God to man, but instead is a series of religious musings containing contradictions and taken from different ancient sources found in other religions of the day. How do you answer this kind of criticism? For a well-researched response, read* Was the New Testament Influenced by Pagan Religions? *by Dr. Ronald H. Nash, located at www.summit.org/Resources/NT&PaganRel.htm.*

WEEK 2, DAY 5

OF ANTS AND UNCLES AND SONS

AN ANT STORY FROM UNCLE NED

Uncle Ned used to tell the story about an anthill that was out by his barn. He would tell it something like this:

> *Sometimes in the evening as the sun was starting to set, I would stroll out to the barn to check on the horses and enjoy the beauty of the sunset as it sprayed a golden glow across the wheat fields.*
>
> *One evening as I was leaning against the barn admiring the magnificent sunset, I looked down and noticed an anthill. I began to study the ants as they scurried around the ground in front of me. As I watched, one little ant crawled up onto my boot, ran across the toe and off the other side. I thought to myself, "What a bold little fellow." He didn't even seem to realize that a being superior to himself existed.*
>
> *As I watched that little ant work, I wondered who put such boldness into so small a creature, and I wondered if I, too, was nothing more than a little ant.*
>
> *Later on that summer, the weather got very hot and the fields became very dry. One afternoon, a thunderstorm hit our area. It came with lots of lightening but little rain. Suddenly, a streak of lightening hit the barn and within seconds there was a raging fire. I hurried to get the animals out of the barn before it was too late. As I rounded the barn, I noticed the anthill and all the ants in their usual busy-ness. I thought, I hate to see those little guys fry in this fire, but there was no way that I could tell them of the impending danger to their home. If there was only some way that I could communicate to those creatures, but the only way that would happen would be for me to become one of them. Then I could communicate to them in "ant" language.*

What is the message of this story?

_____

GOD'S SON SPEAKS OUR LANGUAGE

The most extraordinary thing about God's special revelation is that it involves a person. Jesus Christ was God's specific message to mankind. He became one of us so that He could communicate to us in our language on a personal level.

Yesterday, we discovered several lines of evidence demonstrating that the Bible is inspired. But there is another major reason for believing that the Bible is from God: It is the source that tells us about the special revelation of Jesus. Notice **Hebrews 1:1-3:**

> *Long ago God spoke to the fathers by the prophets at different times and in different ways. ²In these last days, He has spoken to us by His Son, whom He has appointed heir of all things and through whom He made the universe. ³He is the radiance of His glory, the exact expression of His nature, and He sustains all things by His powerful word. After making purification for sins, He sat down at the right hand of the Majesty on high.*

Colossians 2:9-10

For in Him the entire fullness of God's nature dwells bodily, ¹⁰and you have been filled by Him, who is the head over every ruler and authority.

If you want to know what God is like, look at Jesus. Jesus is the exact image or mirror of His Father.

Other "sacred" writings do not give a true picture of the world. Even though they may have some similarities with the moral teaching of Jesus, the writings of the Hindus, Muslims, and Buddhists are much different from the Bible and the teachings of Jesus. And only the Bible accurately describes Christ as the image of God Himself.

CONSIDER THIS!
Are you letting other people's ideas cause you to have doubts about Jesus being God?

❒ Yes

❒ No

If you are not sure that Jesus is truly God, then you'll have a hard time understanding other aspects of a biblical worldview. A biblical Christian view of life is founded on the deity of Jesus. He gives ultimate meaning to life.

Review Colossians 2:9-10. Take a few minutes to think about how these verses apply to you. How does believing this truth affect your relationship with

. . . God:

. . . your parents:

. . . your brothers or sisters:

. . . your friends:

DAY 5 SUMMARY

What did God do to make sure we would understand who He is and that He cares about us?

_____

WEEK 2 SUMMARY: THEOLOGY

The study of theology asks the question: What about God? The Bible reveals that God is not playing hide-and-seek with us when it comes to knowing Him. Everything in the natural universe (general revelation), everything in the Bible (special revelation), and everything about Jesus Christ makes it abundantly clear that God is ruler (He has all power), God is righteous (He is morally perfect), and God is relational (He loves us).

WEEK 3: PHILOSOPHY

GETTING DOWN TO REALITY

"Thinking is the hardest work there is,
which is the probable reason why so few engage in it."
– Henry Ford, 1929*

Want to see your friends' eyeballs roll back in their heads? Ask them this question: "What is life all about?" Many people start rolling their eyes and opening their mouths in wide yawns when the subject of "philosophy" comes up. They say, "Get real! What does philosophy have to do with LIFE?"

Maybe you've even given a sideways glance at the thought of such an impractical subject as philosophy. But, actually, you do have a philosophy, a way of understanding yourself and how you fit into the rest of the world.

Philosophy is the starting point for everything else you do. The way you behave begins with the way you think about life—your philosophy! Yet, if you're like most people today, your philosophy of life is not thought out very clearly.

Therefore, if you want to GET REAL, philosophy starts you in the right direction by asking: "What IS real, and how do I know what is real?"

This week, you will:

▼ Be hungry for some real wisdom

▼ Recognize that everybody believes in something

▼ Learn why the Bible is the source for truth

▼ Make the connection between the reliability of the Scriptures and the resurrection of Jesus

So don't just sit there rolling your eyes, jump into the first day's session!

*Quoted in *How to be Your Own Selfish Pig*, Susan Schaeffer Macaulay, p.15

WEEK 3, DAY 1

HOW REAL IS THE REAL WORLD?

QUESTION: What do you get when you cross a praying mantis with a termite?

ANSWER: A bug that says grace before eating your house!

You see? The termite changes the way it eats your house based on its view of God. Theology really does relate to everyday life!

Last week, you discovered that understanding the basis of any worldview begins with answering the question, "What about God?" This week, you'll explore how your theology relates to another worldview category—philosophy.

WHAT'S THE QUESTION?

In the popular sci-fi film *The Matrix*, the main character, Neo, is consumed with the question, "What is the Matrix?" The Matrix represents people's perception of reality which, as it turns out, is not real at all but a computer-generated image. The plot captures the viewer's imagination because everyone identifies with Neo's question: What is real?

As you think about "reality," what are two or three major questions most people have about their lives?

1) _____
2) _____
3) _____

However someone may state them, the questions can pretty much be broken down into three "standard" *BIG* questions about life:

. . . Where did I come from?

. . . Why am I here?

. . . Where am I going?

Whether you recognize it or not, the way you answer these questions affects every area of your life. And you'll be amazed at how encouraging it can be to build your life on intelligent, well-thought-through answers to these "biggies."

DON'T BE TAKEN INTO CAPTIVITY!

WEEK 3 KEY VERSE

> Colossians 2:8 *Be careful that no one takes you captive through philosophy and empty deceit based on human tradition, based on the elemental forces of the world, and not based on Christ.*

This week's key verse warns against being taken _____ through deceitful philosophies. What might be the results when someone is captured by a deceitful philosophy?

_____

_____

UNDERSTANDING THE TIMES

In contrast to being captured by the world's philosophies, the Bible records the story of a small band, the tribe of Issachar, whose leaders had a unique ability that made them especially valuable to King David. They "understood the times and knew what Israel should do" (**1 Chronicles 12:32**).

Because these leaders had a clear understanding of the _____, they were able to take the right course of action.

In the same way today, God calls Christians to understand the culture of our times so we won't be captured by its philosophies.

FOOD FOR THOUGHT

"Philosophy" [Greek: **philo** (love) + **sophia** (wisdom)] is defined as: The love of wisdom; the attempt to discover an explanation for the whole of existence or reality.

Wisdom gives us a hunger to understand God's design for living. And through philosophy, we seek to know and understand the way the world is designed to work, then to live according to that design. Jesus said, *"Blessed are those who hunger and thirst for righteousness..."* (**Matthew 5:6**).

Spend the next few minutes reflecting on a portion of "wisdom literature" from the Bible, a chapter from the book of Proverbs. Use the space below to answer the following questions: What is the main point that the writer is making? What is the result if you follow the advice?

The main point: (verses 1-5)

_____

_____

_____

_____

_____

The result in your life: (verses 6-10)

_____

_____

_____

_____

_____

DAY 1 SUMMARY

What will happen if you do not base your life on a well-thought-out philosophy?

_____

_____

_____

Proverbs 2

My son, if you accept my words and store up my commands within you, [2]listening closely to wisdom and directing your heart to understanding; [3]furthermore, if you call out to insight and lift your voice to understanding, [4]if you seek it like silver and search for it like hidden treasure, [5]then you will understand the fear of the LORD and discover the knowledge of God. [6]For the LORD gives wisdom; from His mouth come knowledge and understanding. [7]He stores up success for the upright; He is a shield for those who live with integrity [8]so that He may guard the paths of justice and protect the way of His loyal followers. [9]Then you will understand righteousness, justice, and integrity—every good path. [10]For wisdom will enter your heart, and knowledge will delight your soul. [11]Discretion will watch over you, and understanding will guard you, [12]rescuing you from the way of evil — from the one who says perverse things, [13]from those who abandon the right paths to walk in ways of darkness, [14]from those who enjoy doing evil and celebrate evil perversions, [15]whose paths are crooked, and whose tracks are devious. [16]It will rescue you from a forbidden woman, from a stranger with her flattering talk, [17]who abandons the companion of her youth and forgets the covenant of her God; [18]for her house sinks down to death and her ways to the land of the dead. [19]None return who go to her; none attain the paths of life. [20]Therefore, you must walk in the way of the good and keep to the paths of the righteous. [21]For the upright will inhabit the land, and those of integrity will remain in it; [22]but the wicked will be cut off from the land, and the treacherous uprooted from it.

WEEK 3, DAY 2

EVERYBODY'S GOTTA BELIEVE SOMETHING

Think about what a typical college student goes through. It's the first day of Biology 101. As the class begins, Professor Matson clears his throat and introduces the course with this little speech:

> *This semester in biology we'll study the world of living things. During the course of our study, we will discuss the origins of life. These lessons will bring us to that subject some of you religiously inclined ones may not like, the "e" word—evolution. But I can't help that. Evolution is a scientific fact that explains the way life came about and developed on planet earth. We are here to study serious scientific laws and theories. I don't want to hear any of your religious talk about God in this class!*

How do you respond to Professor Matson's remarks? Does religion have a place in a discussion of the origin of life?

_____

NATURE IS NOT NATURALISM!

"Nature" refers to the physical world that we can see, touch, and measure. It's the world of molecules, mud, amoebas, and melons.

But when you add an "ism" to nature, it defines a way of thinking about the whole of reality. It assumes that only stuff that can be physically tested is real. Naturalism presumes that there is no supernatural dimension to life. The fact is, Professor Matson believes in naturalism.

SUPERNATURALISM AND REALITY

On the other hand, "supernaturalism" is the philosophical view that claims a reality separate from the natural world. Accordingly, there is a natural world *AND* a supernatural world, and together, these two make up reality. But here, we run into a problem.

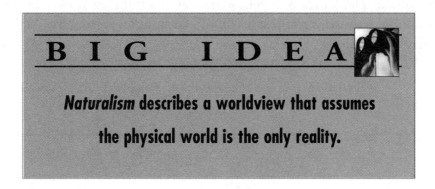

BIG IDEA

Naturalism describes a worldview that assumes the physical world is the only reality.

The basic tenets of Christian philosophy can be demonstrated to be rational, for they are held by average, rational men and women. But surely, Christianity must still run into a... problem. How does the Christian "know" without clashing with science and experience? How can the knowledge we gain through faith in biblical revelation compare to knowledge gained by a scientific investigation of the universe? (TLAC, 36)

Think for a minute about that last question: How does what we know through the Bible compare with what we know from science?

_____

_____

While some people, like Professor Matson, see a clash between the Bible and science, a biblical worldview maintains that there is no disagreement between true scientific discoveries and what the Bible teaches.

EVERYBODY ASSUMES SOMETHING

The basic problem of philosophy is not the problem of faith versus reason. "The crucial problem," says Warren C. Young, "is that some thinkers place their trust in one set of assumptions in their search for truth, while other thinkers place their trust in a quite different set of assumptions." (TLAC, 37)

What are the different sets of assumptions in which people place their trust?

_____

_____

When it comes to learning about reality, the clash is not between science and faith. It is a clash between "faith" in naturalism and "faith" in supernaturalism. Some people start with the belief (a faith assumption) that only nature is real. Christians start with the assumption that God is real.

However, some assumptions are better than others. So the issue comes down to which is the more reasonable assumption? Think back over your journal entries from last week. Remember? **The idea of a supernatural Creator is not just a "blind" faith, but a reasonable, logical conclusion built on everyday observations.**

Based on evidence from the natural world, how would you evaluate Professor Matson's approach to the study of science?

_____

_____

APPLY IT TO YOUR LIFE!

If you begin with the assumption that God is real, it makes sense to seek His wisdom about how you should live. Turn back to Proverbs 2 again, and answer the following question as it is revealed in each of the verses indicated:

What are the benefits of seeking God's wisdom?

v. 11 _____

v. 12 _____

v. 16 _____

v. 20 _____

DAY 2 SUMMARY

Naturalism is a worldview that assumes _____ is the only _____.

What is a better assumption, and why?

_____

_____

 WORLD OF IDEAS ALERT: Take a few minutes to look in the newspaper for articles that relate to the "World of Ideas." Consider the point of view of each in light of today's lesson.

REVIEW KEY VERSE   Colossians 2:8

DIGGING DEEPER: *Explore how naturalism has come to dominate the popular treatment of science in our society today. For a more thorough treatment on the issue of philosophical naturalism see Phillip Johnson's* Reason in the Balance: The Case Against Naturalism in Science, Law & Education, *chapters 2 & 3, or find his article, "The Religion of the Blind Watchmaker," online at www.leaderu.com/real/ri9203/watchmkr.html*

WEEK 3, DAY 3

HOW DO I KNOW WHAT'S TRUE?

TWO SOURCES FOR TRUTH

Yesterday we discovered two ways of looking at reality: naturalism and supernaturalism. So how do we decide which "ism" is right? How do we know which one actually describes reality?

EPISTE-WHAT?!

Epistemology is the discipline that seeks to answer the "how do I know" part of the philosophical question.

When you think about it, there are really only two sources for knowing what is true.

 CONSIDER THIS! You can either believe that truth comes from within yourself or believe in a source outside of yourself.

Why is the first option, "within myself," not the best source for knowing ultimate truth?

_____

_____

That leaves the other option—an outside source. Which of the following serves as an outside source for learning what is true?

(A) My pastor   (E) A philosopher

(B) My parents   (F) Well-known literary works

(C) A professor   (G) A poet

(D) The Bible   (H) Science

Actually, any of the above could serve as a source for learning about reality. But which is the best source? Why?

_____

_____

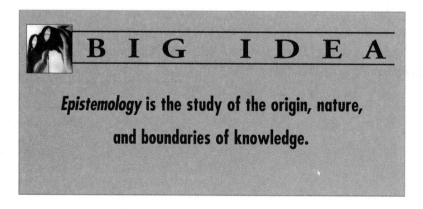

BIG IDEA

Epistemology is the study of the origin, nature, and boundaries of knowledge.

WHOSE SACRED WRITINGS?

If you picked the Bible as the best source for knowing what is real, you're certainly on the right track, but there is still a problem. Your Hindu neighbor says that her sacred writings are the right ones to follow. Muslims also have their own sacred writings (The Qu'ran), and so do Buddhists. For that matter, the Mormons and Jehovah's Witnesses have their versions of the Bible as well as other authoritative sources.

So what makes the Christian Bible so special? Why do Christians say their sacred book is the right one?

> *The evidence in support of the Christian's belief in the divine inspiration of the Bible is convincing. For example, the unity of teaching in the Bible is startling in light of the fact that its books were authored by different men faced with very different circumstances. Further, the astounding ability of the Bible to change the lives of individuals (for the better) who accept its authority strengthens its claim to be a special revelation from God. The degree of moral truth contained in the Bible also supports its divine inspiration. All these arguments support the belief that the Bible is God's Word; however, the most convincing witness for divine inspiration is the Bible itself. Those hesitant to accept Scripture as God's special revelation are most often convinced by a thorough, open-minded study of the Bible.* (TLAC, 22-3)

From the above quotation, list four reasons why the Bible is the ultimate source for truth. Write them in your own words:

(1) _____

(2) _____

(3) _____

(4) _____

Which of the four reasons seems the most convincing to you?
___ Why?

_____

_____

---

2 Timothy 3:16-17

All Scripture is inspired by God and is profitable for teaching, for rebuking, for correcting, for training in righteousness, [17] so that the man of God may be complete, equipped for every good work.

AN INSPIRED BIBLE SHOULD INSPIRE YOU TO ACTION

Take a look at **2 Timothy 3:16-17**, (see page 41).

How does knowing this about Scripture make a difference in your life?

_____

_____

_____

DAY 3 SUMMARY

What are the two possible sources for truth?

(1)_____

(2)_____

REVIEW KEY VERSE

Colossians 2:8 *Be careful that no one takes you captive through philosophy and empty deceit based on human tradition, based on the* _____*of the world, and not based on Christ.*

WEEK 3, DAY 4
THE BIBLE: SOURCE FOR TRUTH

REASONS TO BELIEVE

"You shouldn't question the Bible, should you?" Susan asked thoughtfully. "I mean, aren't we just supposed to believe what it says? But if that's so, why do I have so many questions? Why do I sometimes doubt the Bible is true? I don't know if I can believe all those stories or not."

Susan is not alone in her questioning. Many people have similar thoughts. How would you answer her questions about the Bible?

TESTS FOR TRUTH

Christian philosophy does not throw out reason or tests for truth. Christianity says the New Testament is true because its truths can be tested...[It considers certain] historical evidences that reason itself can employ, much as an attorney [builds a case using evidences to determine questions of fact.] Christian epistemology is based on special revelation which, in turn, is based on history, the law of evidence, and the science of archaeology (TLAC, 37-8).

The above paragraph says that Christian epistemology is based on s_____ r_____. What are three areas of study that support the belief that the Bible is true?

1) _____

2) _____

3) _____

THE HISTORICAL EVIDENCE

What are the chances of this?

If you took 40 different people, living in different places, centuries apart, writing in different moods, coming from different continents, and writing in three different languages about many of the most controversial topics known to man, and put all of their writings together, which would you expect to have? (Check your answer)

❏ A unified, harmonious story.

❏ A jumbled assortment of conflicting ideas.

But the Bible was written in just that way (fill in the blanks from the above paragraph),

by 40 different _____: soldiers, shepherds, statesmen, common men, and kings,

living in different _____: the desert, palaces, small towns, large cities,

_____ apart: periods of war and times of peace; times of prosperity and times of need,

in different _____: feelings of great joy and of great sorrow; moments of fear and times of security,

from different _____: in Egypt (Africa), Judea and Italy (Europe),

in three different _____: Hebrew, Greek and Aramaic,

about controversial _____: the nature of God, moral issues, political alliances, religious ceremonies.

Proverbs 3:1-4
My son, don't forget my teaching, but let your heart keep my commands; [2]*for they will add to you many days, a full life, and well-being.* [3]*Never let loyalty and faithfulness leave you. Tie them around your neck; write them on the tablet of your heart.* [4]*Then you will find favor and high regard in the sight of God and man.*

Yet the Bible is not a mix of contradictory ideas. It reads like one story with harmony and continuity from Genesis to Revelation.

The historical evidence demonstrates that the Bible is one of a kind. It is different from any other religious literature in the way it was written.

CONSIDER THIS!

The Bible is also unique in its ability to change the lives of those who read it and do what it says.

Read the suggested verses from Proverbs 3. Write down the instruction and the benefit that you receive for following the wise advice.

Proverbs 3:1-4

v. 1-2 Wise advice: _____

Personal benefit: _____

v. 3-4 Wise advice: _____

Personal benefit: _____

DAY 4 SUMMARY:

Explain why it makes sense to believe the Bible as a source of knowledge.

_____

_____

_____

_____

_____

WEEK 3, DAY 5

THE BIBLE: HISTORY AND HIS STORY

THE BIBLE BEFORE THE COURT OF LEGAL EVIDENCE

"Legal evidence" refers to principles for proof of something that apply in a court of law. To verify if a crime took place at a particular time in the past, what types of evidence might you expect to see used in court?

_____

_____

In a similar way, the Bible claims to be a key witness testifying to the existence of God. As a historical document, it can be cross-examined to determine its reliability.

IS THE BIBLE RELIABLE?

Since the original documents of the Bible are no longer around, how do we know that valuable information has not been lost in the translations handed down from generation to generation?

When dealing with any ancient document such as the Bible, researchers evaluate two things:

(1) What is the time-interval between the original work and our earliest copy? The copies in hand are dated to determine how long it has been since the original writing. Why would it be important to know this?

_____

(2) How many copies do we have? Then, researchers count the total number of copies available. Why would this matter?

_____

This type of information is called "bibliographic" evidence.

EVIDENCE FOR THE BIBLE

Let's compare the New Testament with several other works of antiquity. (NOTE: The following are just a few of many examples that could be cited.)

1) Caesar wrote a history of the Gallic wars around 58-50 B.C.   There are only 9 or 10 good copies, the oldest being 900 years later than Caesar's day.

2) Livy's history of Rome was written from 59 B.C. to A.D. 17. We only have 20 partial manuscript copies, with only one dating within 400 years of the original.

3) For the New Testament, there are over 14,000 manuscript copies; some within just 250 to 300 years after the original documents were written with fragments as early as 100 to 150 years!

Based on the above evidence, what would you conclude about the Bible compared to other historic writings?

_____

_____

The Bible scholar John Warwick Montgomery concludes: "to be skeptical of the resultant text of the New Testament books is to allow all of classical antiquity to slip into obscurity, for no documents of the ancient period are as well attested bibliographically as the New Testament."[1]

> ## 1 Corinthians 15:5-8
>
> . . . He [Christ] appeared to Cephas, then to the Twelve. [6]Then He appeared to over five hundred brothers at one time, most of whom remain to the present, but some have fallen asleep. [7]Then He appeared to James, then to all the apostles. [8]Last of all, as to one abnormally born, He also appeared to me.

THE RESURRECTION FACTOR

In court, eyewitness testimony is important. How does this relate to the Bible?

Paul writes that the resurrection was positive proof that Jesus was the true Son of God. Notice what he says in **1 Corinthians 15:5-8**. See the references to real people who saw Jesus alive after His crucifixion? Make a list of all those mentioned:

_____

_____

This kind of evidence would stand up in any court of law. The historical eyewitness testimony leads to the conclusion that Jesus actually was raised from the dead. And if this is true, then we need to pay attention to what Jesus said about what's important in life. Jesus stated, *"I am the way, the truth, and the life. No one comes to the Father except through me."* (**John 14:6**)

How have you applied Jesus' statement to your life?

_____

DAY 5 SUMMARY

Why should we have confidence that the Bible is reliable?

_____

_____

 ## THE WORLD OF IDEAS ALERT

If you haven't already done so this week, take a few minutes to look in a newspaper or news magazine for articles that relate to the "World of Ideas." Consider how the Bible might address some of the issues raised.

REVIEW KEY VERSE

Colossians 2:8 *Be careful that no one takes you captive through philosophy and empty deceit based on human tradition, based on the elemental forces of the world, and not* _____.

WEEK 3 SUMMARY

Philosophy asks the questions: "What is real?" and "How do I know?" A biblical worldview states that reality consists of both the natural universe and the supernatural realm. Knowledge comes from a study of both the physical world and God's Word. Because the evidences for the reliability of the Bible are convincing, we conclude that the Bible is the ultimate source of wisdom and knowledge, and we can draw principles for wise living from the Bible. *"In Him all the treasures of wisdom and knowledge are hidden."* (Colossians 2:3)

ENDNOTES

1. John W. Montgomery, *History and Christianity* (Downers Grove, IL.: InterVarsity Press, 1971), p.29.

WEEK 4: BIOLOGY

"DESIGNED" OR "EVOLVED"?

For more than 140 years the issue of how life arose on earth has been hotly debated from high school biology classrooms to state and U.S. supreme courts. What's a Christian to think in light of the conflicting arguments? Some argue the point when the subject of evolution comes up. Others buy into the idea of evolution and begin to doubt the biblical account of creation. Still others throw up their hands with a "Who cares?!" attitude.

But what you believe about the origin of life does matter. It determines not only how you think about biology, but also how you think about every other worldview category. For example, your view on the origin of human life has significant implications for how you understand human psychology. Are we a little "higher" than the apes (according to evolutionary theory) or a little "lower" than the angels (see **Psalm 8:5** on page 51)?

Your journey this week will take you into the biblical worldview of life's origins. You will explore:

▼ The difference between evolutionary theory and "Intelligent Design"

▼ How the biblical worldview is the foundation for modern science

▼ Why the two main principles of evolution—spontaneous generation and natural selection—do not validate evolutionary theory

▼ Why an Intelligent Designer (God) is the only scientifically possible solution in the origin-of-life debate

WEEK 4, DAY 1

CREATION OR EVOLUTION

WHAT DOES IT MATTER?

Every nightly news program highlighted the story. Papers ran front-page articles. And radio talk shows rattled on about the Kansas Board of Education when it voted to eliminate some of the questions about evolution from the state's competency tests. At your part-time job, a co-worker corners you in the break room and says:

> *What's all the fuss about over the Kansas thing? I don't see the big problem. Can't we just teach everybody about plants and animals and not worry about how they got here? What difference does it make if God created life or if it started in some "primordial soup" billions of years ago? The fact is, we're here. Let's just get on with life!*

How would you respond? Does it matter what you believe about the origin of life? Explain your answer.

_____

_____

The theory of evolution states that all life came about by impersonal forces operating by chance over 3.5 billion years without any intervention from God.

If evolution is true, what are the implications concerning the following areas:

God:

_____

Human nature:

_____

Ethical standards:

_____

WHAT A DIFFERENCE IT MAKES!

If Darwinian evolution is true, then God had nothing to do with the origin of life. Nature did not need His help to bring about the first life or all the subsequent species of plants and animals living today. Therefore, "God" is nothing more than a concept that primitive man developed to try to understand the mysteries of life.

As far as human nature is concerned, evolution describes mankind as the highest form of living organism. It assumes that we are basically good and getting better all the time. There is no sin problem marring our basic instincts.

And related to ethics, Darwin's theory implies that concepts of right and wrong are simply social constructs that have developed over time and are constantly changing to fit the evolutionary progress of the human species. Morals are relative and situational.

How does this view contrast with a biblical perspective?

_____

BUT WHAT ABOUT . . .

Some Christians object to the above implications of Darwinism by saying that God could have used the process of evolution to bring about life. This is called *theistic evolution.*

Theistic evolutionists contend that the term "creation" simply means that God created the first spark of life and then directed His creation through the vehicle of gradual evolution.

So what's so bad about that?

[Hint: Jacques Monod and Bertrand Russell, both evolutionists, refer to evolution as a wasteful, cruel process (elimination of the weakest species, etc.).]

Psalm 8:5
You made him [mankind] little less than God, and crowned him with glory and honor.

> ### Genesis 1:31
>
> And God saw all He had made, and it was very good. Evening came, and then morning: a sixth day.

> ### John 1:1-3
>
> In the beginning was the Word; and the Word was with God, and the Word was God. [2]He was with God in the beginning. [3]All things were created through Him, and apart from Him not one thing was created that has been created.

Is this a picture of how the God of the Bible initiated life (see **Genesis 1:31**; **John 1:1-3**)?

_____

_____

THE WORLDVIEW CONNECTION

Theistic evolution has a serious problem because it tries to mix two conflicting worldviews. A biblical worldview has definite implications about the origin of life as created by God (theology), provides a specific understanding of mankind (psychology), and offers a clear view of what is moral (ethics). Once you see the connections between these seemingly different categories, you are thinking based on a total worldview.

Evolutionary theory also has implications for these same areas but comes to vastly different conclusions because it is based on a worldview contrary to that of the Bible.

For people who believe in evolution, the philosophical starting point is naturalism. You'll remember from our Week 3, Day 2 discussion that this worldview assumes there is no God and that the sum total of reality is the material universe. There is no supernatural. It is out of these beliefs that their theories of the nature and role of science are constructed.

THEOLOGICAL DIFFERENCES

The two views of origins, Intelligent Design and Darwinian evolution, also have very different implications concerning the nature of mankind.

> More important, if evolution is true, then the story of the Garden of Eden and original sin must be viewed as nothing more than allegory, a view that undermines the significance of Christ's sinless life and sacrificial death on the cross. . . . If Adam was not a historical individual, and if his

fall into sin was not historical, then the biblical doctrines of sin and of Christ's atonement for it collapse. (TLAC, 50)

In your own words, state the problem presented:

_____

You can see, then, that how one answers the question of biology reflects a total world and life view, one that begins with theology and progresses through philosophy before arriving at biology. We cannot escape the implications concerning that foundational question of God.

REFLECTING ON GOD'S CREATION

Spend a few minutes reading **Psalm 19:1-6**. Then, pause and thank God for His power in creating the beauty of this world and pray for His help in grasping a worldview consistent with His revelation.

DAY 1 SUMMARY

What makes Darwinian evolution and design theory incompatible?

_____

_____

WEEK 4 KEY VERSES

Colossians 1:16-17 *Because by Him [Christ] everything was created, in heaven and on earth, the visible and the invisible, whether thrones or dominions or rulers or authorities—all things have been created through Him and for Him.* [17] *He is before all things, and by Him all things hold together.*

> ## Psalm 19:1-6
>
> *The heavens declare the glory of God, and the sky proclaims the work of His hands.*
> [2] *Day after day they pour out speech; night after night they communicate knowledge.*
> [3] *There is no speech; there are no words; their voice is not heard.*
> [4] *Their message has gone out to all the earth, and their words to the ends of the inhabited world.*
> *In the heavens He has pitched a tent for the sun.*
> [5] *It is like a groom coming from the bridal chamber; it rejoices like an athlete running a course.*
> [6] *It rises from one end of the heavens and circles to their other end; nothing is hidden from its heat.*

WEEK 4, DAY 2

SCIENCE AND RELIGION

THINGS THAT GO TOGETHER

Chocolate chip cookies and ice cold milk—a great combo! They just naturally go together. List three other pairs of things that go together:

(1)

(2)

(3)

Summertime and vacations, Thanksgiving and turkey, fall Fridays and football. Connections are made between each pair because we are accustomed to having them in combination.

But what about science and religion? Do they go together? Many people consider these two fields of study totally incompatible.

MODERN SCIENCE AND THE BIBLE

> *The roots of modern science are grounded in a Christian view of the world. This is not surprising, since science is based on the assumption that the universe is orderly and can be expected to act according to specific, discoverable laws. An ordered, lawful universe would seem to be the effect of an intelligent Cause, which was precisely the belief of many early scientists.* (TLAC, 51)

What does the above text say about the religious foundation of modern science?

_____

_____

What is it about biblical Christianity that forms the basis for studying the world of nature?

_____

_____

FOUNDERS OF MODERN SCIENCE

Do religion and science go together? The early "modern" scientists founded the principles of science that we still use today. Read what some of them have to say on the subject of religion and science.

Johannes Kepler (1571-1630) is the founder of modern astronomy. He demonstrated that the sun is the center of the solar system, published the first tables for tracking star motions, and contributed to the development of calculus.

He states that in his scientific research he was merely "thinking God's thoughts after Him." What do you think Kepler meant by that?

_____

_____

Robert Boyle (1627-1691) is called the father of modern chemistry. He was also a diligent student of the Bible and gave much of his own money to the work of Bible translation.

Do you imagine that Boyle saw a problem between his study of chemistry and his belief in God? Why not?

_____

_____

Isaac Newton (1642-1727) discovered the law of universal gravitation, formulated the three laws of motion, and developed calculus into a comprehensive branch of mathematics. He constructed the first reflecting telescope. And he wrote books on biblical subjects as well as papers refuting atheism and defending creation and the Bible. Regarding the solar system, Newton writes:

> *This most beautiful system of sun, planets, and comets could only proceed from the counsel and dominion of an intelligent and powerful Being.*[1]

Did Newton's strong belief in God help or hinder his ability to be involved in useful scientific inquiry and discovery?

_____

_____

SEARCH FOR "THE WORLD OF IDEAS"

Take a few minutes to search the newspaper to look for signs of "intelligent life" on planet earth.

IF YOU ARE A PART OF A GROUP STUDY: Bring an article or idea to the next group meeting and share with everyone the worldview being presented.

IF YOU ARE STUDYING INDIVIDUALLY: Write a brief paragraph explaining the worldview of five articles.

DAY 2 SUMMARY

Write a brief summary concerning how science and religion interface.

_____

_____

_____

_____

WEEK 4, DAY 3
MODERN SCIENCE AND CREATION

LIVING IN THE 21ST CENTURY

After telling a friend what you are learning about the early modern scientists and their biblical worldview, he responds,

> Sure, that may have been true for those guys 300 years ago, but face it, science has discovered a lot since then. We no longer need "God" to explain how things work. Science has demonstrated that life could evolve on its own without His help.

Does your friend have a well-founded point? Is the worldview of the early scientists still valid today? Is there evidence of design and a Designer, or have we gained new, scientific knowledge that would allow us to reject the biblical view of a Creator?

_____

_____

RELEARNING OLD LESSONS

> Science is re-learning an old lesson: the more one discovers about the universe, the more one discovers design. Many notable scientists . . . describe the design in nature revealed to them through science. Physicist Paul Davies, who does not profess to be a Christian, supports. . . creationism when he says, "Every advance in fundamental physics seems to uncover yet another facet of order." At first, this seems to be an obvious conclusion of little significance. But strict evolution demands chance rather than a Law-maker as the guiding force. When a world-class non-Christian scientist like Davies declares that the universe cannot be viewed as a product of chance, it is a severe blow to materialistic evolutionary theory. (TLAC, 52-3)

What is the point that physicist Paul Davies makes?

_____

_____

How does this contradict strict evolutionary theory?

_____

_____

MODERN SCIENTISTS

Not only did the early modern scientists believe in a God who created life and the cosmos, many top scientists in our own generation believe the same thing. To get an idea of how some of the best scientists today relate religion and science, check out the following quotes:

Wernher von Braun (1912-1977) was one of the world's top space scientists. A leading German rocket engineer, he migrated to the United States and became director of NASA. He writes:

> *Manned space flight is an amazing achievement, but it has opened for mankind thus far only a tiny door for viewing the awesome reaches of space. An outlook through this peep-hole at the vast mysteries of the universe should only confirm our belief in the certainty of its Creator. I find it ... difficult to understand a scientist who does not acknowledge the presence of a superior rationality behind the existence of the universe...*[2]

What did viewing the "vast mysteries of the universe" lead von Braun to conclude about the existence of God?

_____

_____

Professor Henry Margenau, professor of physics for over 40 years at Yale University, has received 8 honorary doctorate degrees, was a visiting professor at 12 universities, and worked with Albert Einstein. He says:

> *If you ask scientists who have a mild training in science...you do get the impression that there is a conflict between science and religion. But if you ask really good scientists...leading scientists, the people who have made contributions which have made science grow so vastly in the last fifty years, [these scientists] are... all religious in their beliefs.*[3]

Based on Professor Margenau's comment, the "really good" top scientists around the world see science and religion as having:

❑   some conflict

❑   a lot of conflict

❑   no conflict

There are many other current scientists who could be quoted, but you get the idea from these that there is no basic conflict between the study of science and biblical Christianity.

REALITY AND RATIONALITY

Phillip Johnson, professor of law at U.C. Berkley, states in his book, *Reason in the Balance:*

> *If God really does exist, then to lead a rational life a person has to take account of God and His purposes. A person or a society that ignores the Creator is ignoring the most important part of reality, and to ignore reality is to be irrational.*[4]

Look again at Psalm 19:1-5 (*Week 4, Day 1*). The writer of this psalm makes the rational connection between the Creator and the creation. Reflect on its meaning for your life and our society and note your thoughts here.

_____

_____

_____

_____

_____

DAY 3 SUMMARY

Why do top scientists see no conflict between science and belief in God?

_____

_____

REVIEW KEY VERSES:

> Colossians 1:16-17 *Because by Him [Christ] everything was created, in heaven and on earth, the visible and the invisible, whether thrones or dominions or rulers or authorities—all things have been created* _____ _____ *and* _____ _____. [17]*He is before all things, and by Him all things hold together.*

WEEK 4, DAY 4

SPONTANEOUS GENERATION

"Okay, okay, so there are some scientists today who believe that God has something to do with science and the origin of life," your friend acknowledges. "But I learned in biology class that most scientists think life arose on Earth from inanimate matter. And then in the textbook was an experiment by Stanley Miller demonstrating how the building blocks of life could have formed spontaneously on the early earth. It seems that scientific experiments prove that life could come about without the help of some supernatural Being."

Respond to your friend's comments:

_____

_____

Most high school and college textbooks give only the positive aspects of the above-mentioned experiment by Dr. Miller, leaving out any negative data. For the sake of fairness and honest scientific inquiry, let's see if there is any contrary information concerning these types of experiments.

IN THE "BIG INNING"

First of all, you need to keep in mind that origin-of-life experiments are supposed to be re-enactments of what could have happened in a warm pond on the early earth. But scientists manipulate the experiment in different ways to get the desired results. Let's use the analogy of a baseball game to see how.

It's the bottom of the ninth, the game is tied, and the best "origin-of-life" batter comes to the plate. This is the "Big Inning"!

THE FIRST PITCH: All chemists know that in a real pond there are all sorts of chemical reactions, many of which cancel out the reactions needed for the formation of life. So what does the researcher do? He starts with pure ingredients. But in a natural setting, there is no way to purify the starting materials to get the desired results. The "origin-of-life" batter just swung and missed: "Strike one!"

THE SECOND PITCH: Chemists also know that ultraviolet light from the sun destroys amino acids, the building blocks of life. So in origin-of-life experiments the scientist screens out certain wavelengths of light. However, in a natural setting there would be no filter to remove these deadly rays. That's "Strike two!" against the odds of life originating on its own.

THE THIRD PITCH: A third thing that scientists know is that the building blocks of life (amino acids and proteins) are very delicate and can easily break down into the elemental chemicals that make them up. So the researcher rigs a trap to remove them from the reaction site as soon as they form, to protect them from disintegration. But nature doesn't come with protective traps. In real life, when amino acids form they disintegrate almost immediately. So the experiment misses real life again: "Strike three!"

The umpire looks at the origin-of-life batter and hollers, **"YOU'RE OUT!"**

Actually, origin-of-life experiments have eleven major problems, the three just mentioned plus eight more! And any one of these eleven problems by itself would stop the progress from non-living molecules to living cells.

Based on the above "batting average," what can you say concerning the idea of "spontaneous generation"?

_____

_____

_____

_____

GOD HITS A HOME RUN!

> *Dean Kenyon, a biochemist and a former chemical evolutionist, now writes, "When all relevant lines of evidence are taken into account, and all the problems squarely faced, I think we must conclude that life owes its inception to a source outside of nature."*
> (TLAC, 55)

Professor Dean Kenyon is also co-author of a popular college textbook on chemistry and so knows a great deal about the origin of life. Dr. Kenyon concludes that the evidence clearly points to life coming from . . .

❑ a warm pond + natural processes

❑ another planet

❑ a supernatural source.

"LIFE ONLY COMES FROM . . ."

Take a biology textbook used in most schools today, and look back several pages from the chapter on evolution. You probably will find that the knowledge of where life comes from was determined by another scientist in 1860, the year after Darwin published his famous theory on evolution, and that the conclusion doesn't fit very well with Darwin's theory.

People had long thought that life could generate itself from non-living matter. They pointed to such things as frogs emerging from the mud of riverbanks as evidence for this idea. But in 1860, Louis Pasteur ended this belief, called spontaneous generation, by a series of scientific experiments which proved that "life only comes from pre-existing life." His experiments have been verified over the years and never contradicted.

How does Pasteur's scientific conclusion compare with current evolutionary theory? You could chart it this way:

SCIENCE SAYS   EVOLUTION SAYS

"Life comes from life"   "Life comes from non-life"

What do you notice as you compare these two statements?

_____

Which statement has been proven scientifically to be true?

_____

Since the two statements are contradictory, if one is true, what would the other be?

    ❒   True

    ❒   False

 CONSIDER THIS!

The most basic premise of Darwinian evolution—the idea that "life comes from non-life"–is, scientifically, a false statement!

If evolution is not based on scientific observations, then what is it based on? It is founded on naturalism, the religious assumption we explored on Week 3, Day 2. In contrast, the biblical worldview states what science has confirmed:

"Life only comes from life!"

Read **Genesis 1:1, 11, 20 and 2:7** to find out the most scientifically accurate statement you can make regarding the origin of life: "In the beginning, _____ _____ . . ."

DAY 4 SUMMARY

Why is evolution a scientific impossibility?

Because _____ only comes from _____.

Genesis 1:1, 11, 20, 2:7

1:1 In the beginning God created the heavens and the earth.

1:11 And God said, "Let the earth produce vegetation: seed-bearing plants, and fruit trees on the earth bearing fruit, with seed in it, according to their kind." And it was so.

1:20 Then God said, "Let the water swarm with living creatures, and let birds fly above the earth across the expanse of the sky."

2:7 Then the LORD God shaped the man from the dust of the ground and breathed the breath of life into his nostrils, and the man became a living being.

WEEK 4, DAY 5
AFTER THEIR KIND . . .

WHAT DO CORN, COWS AND CATS PROVE?

Your friend sure is persistent. He is convinced that science has proven evolution true.

After talking with him about the problems with the origin-of-life experiments, he changes the subject:

> *But look at all of the evidence for evolution. I mean, take natural selection, for example. Scientists have conducted breeding experiments to produce sweeter corn, cows that give more milk, and cats with fluffier fur. If a breeder can select for certain traits, then nature can select changes for the better. So natural selection proves evolution!*

Has your friend made a good point this time? How do you respond to his argument for natural selection creating new species?

_____

_____

BIRD'S BEAKS AND EVOLUTION

Darwin made a now-famous voyage to the Galapagos Islands where he discovered on the various islands finches whose beak sizes differed slightly. He thought he had discovered evolution in action. But had he?

Darwin's theory of evolution assumes that all of the diversity of life came from simpler, less complex forms of life. You might call it the "amoeba-to-man" theory.

For this "amoeba-to-man" idea to actually work, new complex structures must emerge. Let's face it, a man is much more complex than an amoeba! *For evolution to occur you have to "add new stuff."*

So, did Darwin observe any "new stuff" being added to the birds? No. Darwin only observed small changes in the size of the finches' beaks, not the addition of new features. What Darwin called "natural selection" was actually "adaptation," the process whereby animals can change slightly to adapt to their environment. But these small adaptive changes have never been observed to lead to whole new structures.

The same thing is true for other examples given in most biology textbooks. Even the famous "peppered moth" experiment begins with moths and ends with moths. No new features were ever added! This is adaptation, but not evolution the way Darwin envisioned.

CREATOR TO THE RESCUE

Look at Genesis 1:12, 21, 25, and you will notice that God created various plants and animals "according to their _____."

The phrase "according to their kind" suggests that the boundary between kinds is defined by reproduction: a "kind" is an interbreeding group.

For example, the entire cat family, from domestic cats to leopards and tigers, forms a breeding chain and hence constitutes a single "kind." So does the dog family, from our friendly beagles to wolves and even jackals.

WINGS ON PIGS!

> Edward Deevey, Jr. [has written] "Some remarkable things have been done by crossbreeding and selection inside the species barrier, or within a larger circle of closely related species, such as the wheats. But wheat is still wheat, and not, for instance, grapefruit; and we can no more grow wings on pigs than hens can make cylindrical eggs." (TLAC, 58)

Does natural selection prove Darwinian evolution? Write your conclusion regarding the concept of natural selection based on the best scientific observations:

_____

_____

_____

Genesis 1:12, 21, 25

1:12 The land brought forth vegetation: seed-bearing plants according to their kind and trees bearing fruit with seed in it, according to their kind. And God saw that it was good.

1:21 So God created the large sea-creatures and all living creatures that move and swarm in the water, according to their kinds. He also created every winged bird according to its kind. And God saw that it was good.

1:25 So God made the wildlife of the earth according to their kinds, and the livestock according to their kinds, and creatures that crawl on the ground according to their kinds. And God saw that it was good.

EVOLUTION, CREATION AND FAITH

The belief that God created all things, including man in His own image, requires faith. But evolutionary theory requires more faith, since evolution runs contrary to reason, science and history. (TLAC, 63)

What is the difference between faith in a Creator and faith in evolution?

_____

_____

DAY 5 SUMMARY

How does adaptation differ from natural selection?

_____

_____

WEEK 4 SUMMARY:

How you view the origin of life matters! An unbiased study of biology leads to the following conclusions:

(1) Living organisms show incredible evidence of "design,"

(2) Life only comes from pre-existing life, and

(3) Living things reproduce only after their own kind.

The most scientific statement you can make concerning the origin of life is: "In the beginning God created it!"

Review each day's assignment for this week. Which ideas were most significant to you? Why?

_____

_____

Spend some time in praise to God for His awesome power and wisdom in creating this diverse world of beautiful living things.

ACTION POINT!

Invite a group of friends over for pizza and a discussion of the ideas from this week's study on biology. It will help them think through the issues and evaluate what they hear in biology class and through the media. And if they are not Christians, it will demonstrate the logical basis for believing in an Intelligent Designer. Pray about it, and go for it!

DIGGING DEEPER: *The "neo-Darwinian" theory states that natural selection works on chance mutations in the genes to produce novel features in the offspring. Check out why mutations do not provide the necessary material for unlimited change (macroevolution) in a species. One particularly good resource is* The Natural Limits to Biological Change, *by Lane Lester and Raymond Bohlin (check online at www.probe.org/docs/natlim.html for an article about the book).*

ENDNOTES

1. Nancy R. Pearcey and Charles B. Thaxton, *The Soul of Science* (Crossway, Wheaton, IL, 1994), p.91.

2. Henry M. Morris, *Men of Science, Men of God,* (Creation Life Publishers, El Cajon, CA, 1988), p.85.

3. Roy Varghese, *The Intellectuals Speak Out About God* (Regnery Gateway, Chicago, IL,1984), p. 43.

4. Phillip E. Johnson, *Reason in the Balance* (InterVarsity Press, Downers Grove, IL, 1995), p. 7.

N O T E S

WEEK 5: PSYCHOLOGY

HOW TO LIVE WITH YOURSELF AND LIKE IT!

The ideas you have about life determine how much you enjoy life. Are you happy and satisfied? It's because you think that way. Are you sad or depressed? Often those feelings stem from the way you think about yourself.

So what is the source of your thoughts and ideas? Knowing that is crucial to answering the question, "Who are you?"

To find answers, we turn to psychology—the study of the "psyche," or "soul." Psychology seeks an understanding of what you are like on the inside, the place where you do all of your real living.

During this week's journey you will discover:

▼ The biblical view of YOU

▼ Why you don't have to put on an "act" around other people

▼ Your royal heritage as a Christian

▼ How not to be your own selfish pig!

So to enjoy life to the max, start with a new set of ideas from your study of biblical Christian psychology!

WEEK 5, DAY 1
WHO AM I, REALLY?

PSYCHOLOGY, THE BIBLE, AND YOU

Psychology is the study of what makes up the real, inside "you." But isn't psychology a "secular" discipline? How can it be compatible with the Bible? As you're about to find out, the Bible has a lot to say about who you really are.

> *Christianity and psychology are compatible for the simple reason that the worldview of biblical Christianity contains a psychology. As Charles L. Allen aptly points out, "the very essence of religion is to adjust the mind and soul of man. . . . Healing means bringing the person into a right relationship with the physical, mental and spiritual laws of God." Man created "in the image of God" (Genesis 1:27) requires a worldview that recognizes the significance of the spiritual.* (TLAC, 69)

The above text makes an interesting connection between the study of psychology and other worldview categories that we have discussed so far. Match each phrase with the discipline related to it by drawing a line between the two:

"religion"	psychology
"mind and soul of man"	theology
"physical, mental and spiritual laws of God"	biology
"created"	philosophy

The big idea that is emerging from our study is this: There is a connection between each of the worldview disciplines. The Bible builds a whole picture of LIFE, from your understanding of God to how you view yourself.

THE BIBLE'S VIEW OF YOU

Walk into almost any college psychology class and you will be taught that "you" are just a bundle of molecules and electrical impulses. This is called "psychological monism"—referring to a "one-dimensional" view of humankind based on atheistic theology, naturalistic philosophy and evolutionary biology.

However, the Bible reveals a different understanding of man's basic make-up.

Using Jesus' statement in **Matthew 10:28**, answer these questions:

Jesus refers to what two dimensions of life?

_____

_____

What does Jesus say about our bodies?

_____

_____

What does He say about our souls?

_____

_____

What evidence do you see that people consist of a spiritual dimension? (Hint: Ideas and beliefs are not physical entities.)

_____

_____

> ### Matthew 10:28
>
> *Don't fear those who kill the body but are not able to kill the soul; but rather, fear Him who is able to destroy both soul and body in hell.*

DUALISM. . . NO KIDDING!

You are more than just your physical body. And you are more than just a product of natural processes operating over time.

> *The Bible's statements regarding body, breath of life, soul, spirit, and mind suggest a dualist ontology; that is, the view that human nature consists of two fundamental kinds of reality: physical (material or natural) and spiritual (supernatural) . . . The Bible does not deny body; it simply says man is more than body.*
> (TLAC, 69-70)

According to the biblical view, the real "you" consists of . . .

❏ _____ (bones and blood and skin), plus
❏ _____ (a special and unique personality)

TIME TO CELEBRATE!

When it gets down to it, you're special. Your body is not all of you, or even the most important part of you. The "real" you is on the inside of this wonderful body.

Take a few minutes to celebrate this real you. Make a list of the special qualities that God has given you in each of the following areas. (Be sure not to confuse what society is telling you is special with what God thinks.)

Body _____

Soul _____

and don't forget to thank God for making you so special!

DAY 1 SUMMARY

How does the Bible relate to psychology?

_____

_____

WEEK 5 KEY VERSE

Colossians 2:13 *And when you were dead in trespasses and in the uncircumcision of your flesh, He made you alive with Him and forgave us all our trespasses.*

DIGGING DEEPER: *In an appeal for support of higher education, a TV spot used the slogan, "The mind is a terrible thing to waste." But this raises the question, what is the mind? Is consciousness just a function of the brain and nothing more, or is the mind an aspect of an immaterial soul distinct from the body? This is referred to as the "mind/body" problem. Dig deeper into the issue with J. P. Moreland's book,* Scaling the Secular City, *chapter 3, "God and the Argument from Mind." Or, read the article on artificial intelligence by John Beloff found online at:*

www.leaderu.com/truth/2truth04.html.

WEEK 5, DAY 2

GOD'S IMAGE

KATHY'S WORLD

It really shattered my life when my parents' marriage broke up. I was thirteen, and I couldn't get it out of my head that somehow I was responsible for their divorce. Everyone had been so grouchy and disapproving of me for so long that I figured it must be all my fault. . . . As I went through school, I was very mixed up. I felt unsure of myself, so I tried to do anything that I thought would get other kids to accept me. If they were smoking, I'd smoke. If a boy wanted something sexual from me, I'd give it to him. When drugs were passed out, I'd try them. All the time I was really crying, "Am I worth anything to anybody?" [1]

No one would have guessed Kathy felt that way. On the outside she was full of fun. But under that veneer of joy and energy was a deep-seated despair.

Do you know someone like Kathy? _____

Have you ever had some of the same feelings as Kathy? If so, which ones?

_____

_____

Kathy seems to have a problem that goes beyond her parents' divorce. What would that problem be?

_____

_____

Could it be that Kathy wanted to matter as a person, but she had no basic reason for believing that she did? Maybe she had bought into the logical conclusion of an evolutionary worldview that told her she was just another highly developed animal—a thinking, talking, medium-sized biped—taking up space on the planet for a few years.

Kathy cried out, "Am I worth anything to anybody?" If she had said that to you, what would you have said in reply?

_____

_____

Genesis 1:27

So God created man in His own image; He created him in the image of God; He created them male and female.

Psalm 8:4-5

What is man, that You remember him, the son of man, that You look after him? ⁵You made him little less than God, and crowned him with glory and honor.

Psalm 139:13-16

For it was You who created my inward parts; You knit me together in my mother's womb.

¹⁴I will praise You because I am unique in remarkable ways. Your works are wonderful, and I know this very well.

¹⁵My bones were not hidden from You when I was made in secret, when I was formed in the depths of the earth.

¹⁶Your eyes saw me when I was formless; all my days were written in Your book and planned before a single one of them began.

THE TRUEST THINGS ABOUT YOU

Kathy was depressed because she believed she lived in a one-dimensional universe. All she could see was the physical world, the natural realm of existence, her "outer shell." So when her world started to cave in around her, she was left without a means to cope with her feelings of isolation and abandonment.

We learned during our study of biblical philosophy that our universe is not one-dimensional, but two-dimensional. What are the two realms that make up the "totality of reality"?

(1) The N_____ realm

(2) The S_____ realm

Man's spiritual element is his very essence and the element of man on which proper psychology should focus. A psychology that ignores the existence of the spirit cannot hope to deal with the deepest, most profound problems experienced by man.

Secular humanist psychologists ignore the spiritual dimension of life when it comes to dealing with people's personal problems. What do you think might be the results of this denial?

_____

_____

_____

GOD'S IMAGE / MY IMAGE

In contrast to secular humanist psychology, check out what God says about humanity. After each passage, apply the idea to Kathy's life by writing out what you would tell her about who she really is.

Passage	Main Idea	Applied To Kathy
Genesis 1:27		
Psalm 8:4-5		
Psalm 139:13-14		
Psalm 139:15-16		

All of these passages have one very important idea in common. How would you summarize that idea?

_____

_____

What makes you so special is that God has made you in His image. God's image is not found in your body or physical being, but in your mental, moral and spiritual capabilities.

TRUE SELF-ESTEEM

Self-esteem is not produced by just having warm fuzzy thoughts about yourself. It comes as a result of understanding who you really are. And the truest thing about you is what God says about you!

Take another look at those passages that you applied to Kathy's life. Guess what? They apply to your life, too! After each passage, write how the main idea relates to you.

Genesis 1:27 _____

Psalm 8:4-5 _____

Psalm 139:13-14 _____

Psalm 139:15-16 _____

DAY 2 SUMMARY

What is it that gives you worth?

_____

_____

WEEK 5, DAY 3
GREATLY FALLEN

KATHY'S ACTING CAREER

Kathy felt mixed up and unsure of herself, so she turned to acting, pretending to be somebody that she was not. Read how she describes it.

> . . .Like I said, I did anything to get other kids to accept me. If they smoked, I smoked. If a boy wanted something sexual, I gave it. When they passed out drugs, I used them. I tried to look beautiful. I tried to be popular. I tried for top grades, and dreamed of a high-status career. But by the time I got to college, I'd decided that I was a nobody, and life was a big hoax. Everybody was just going through the motions of living, pretending that what they thought and chose really mattered. You could only exist if you put on an act for other people as well as yourself.[2]

Look again at all the ways Kathy used to try to feel better about herself. List each activity under one of the following two headings:

The Good

The Bad

None of those things, even "the good" activities, brought Kathy the happiness and sense of self-worth she longed for. Why not?

_____

_____

Kathy was looking for self-love in all the wrong places. She was faking her inner feelings by projecting an outward character that was not true to her insides. She had ignored the spiritual dimension of her life.

NEGLECTING THE SPIRIT

> _Francis A. Schaeffer sums up: "The basic psychological problem is trying to be what we are not, and trying to carry what we cannot carry. Most of all, the basic problem is not being willing to be the creatures we are before the Creator." (TLAC, 71)_

What do you think Schaeffer meant by describing the basic problem as "not being willing to be the creatures we are before the Creator"?

_____

_____

THE REST OF THE STORY

> *A proper understanding of man's nature does not, however, end with affirming the existence of a spirit within man. The Christian position goes on to define man's nature as inherently evil because of man's decision to disobey God in the garden of Eden. This understanding of man's sinful bent is critical for understanding man's nature and mental processes.* (TLAC, 71)

According to the Christian position, what is the source of our psychological problems?

_____

If our sinful bent is the problem, what is the solution?

_____

_____

BIBLICAL PSYCHOLOGY TO THE RESCUE

These passages describe the process of taking responsibility for your own thoughts and actions. For each set of verses, write an action point applying the passage to your life.

Romans 3:22-26

Colossians 1:13-14

John 1:12

Romans 3:22-26

. . .that is, God's righteousness through faith in Jesus Christ, to all who believe, since there is no distinction. [23] For all have sinned and fall short of the glory of God. [24] They are justified freely by His grace through the redemption that is in Christ Jesus. [25] God presented Him as a propitiation through faith in His blood, to demonstrate His righteousness, because in His restraint God passed over the sins previously committed. [26] He presented Him to demonstrate His righteousness at the present time, so that He would be righteous and declare righteous the one who has faith in Jesus.

Colossians 1:13-14

He rescued us from the domain of darkness and transferred us into the kingdom of the Son He loves, [14] in whom we have redemption, the forgiveness of sins.

John 1:12

But to all who did receive Him, He gave them the right to be children of God, to those who believe in His name.

THE REST OF KATHY'S STORY

As it turns out Kathy came to realize her spiritual condition and her need for God's forgiveness. She bowed her head and said, "Thank you, God. I accept your gift for me." Kathy found a new self-knowledge and an understanding of her personal worth after she accepted God's offer of complete forgiveness. Her "act" was over.[3]

Have you made the wonderful discovery of experiencing God's love and forgiveness? If not, talk with a parent, pastor or Bible study leader about it this week.

If you have already accepted Jesus Christ as your Savior, then thank Him for giving you a new life, inner peace, and the pathway toward a meaningful life!

REVIEW KEY VERSE

Colossians 2:13 *And when you were _____ in trespasses and in the uncircumcision of your _____, He made you alive with Him and _____ us all our trespasses.*

DAY 3 SUMMARY

Why do even good things we do fall short of building up our sense of happiness and self-worth?

_____

_____

WEEK 5, DAY 4
A CHILD OF THE KING

ONCE UPON A TIME . . .

. . . in a distant land, a son was born to the king and queen. But the baby boy was kidnapped and sold to a traveling merchant. A few years later the merchant and his wife died of a fever, leaving the young boy to fend for himself. The boy lived in poverty, begging food and sleeping in little shelters made from sticks.

On the twentieth anniversary of his son's birth, the king summoned his most trusted servant to go out in search of the prince. The servant had gone out many times before but had always come back with no news of the royal son. But at the king's bidding, he set out yet another time to find the son who would now have grown into a man.

At dusk on the third day, the servant stopped to rest his horse beside a clear-flowing stream when a young man came up to beg for bread. As the servant handed him a small loaf from his pack, he noticed an unusual mark on the young man's right hand. It was the birthmark of the prince!

The servant joyously told the beggar about his real identity and took him back to the castle to be united with his royal family. The prince lived happily ever after in the joy and bounty of the royal palace.

Like all fables, this make-believe story teaches us a principle about life. If the baby son represents a newborn Christian, what is the point of the story?

_____

LIVING IN SPIRITUAL POVERTY

The story of the royal son illustrates an important biblical principle. The Bible describes Christians as ". . . a chosen race, a royal priesthood, a holy nation, a people for His possession. . ."
(1 Peter 2:9).

But sometimes, like the son in the story, we are not aware of our royal spiritual heritage, and as a result, live in spiritual "poverty," not experiencing the incredible richness available to us by birthright.

Describe someone living in spiritual "poverty":

_____

_____

THE ROYAL YOU

Although it sometimes happens, a Christian does not have to live in spiritual poverty. Understanding our identity in Christ opens us to experience all the great things God has in store for us.

In the verses below, fill in the blanks to underscore the significant truths about yourself as a child of the King! (You'll find the verses in the "Scripture Supplement" section on pages 85-6. It may seem like a lot to review, but the time you spend will be well worth the effort!)

John 1:12   I am a _____ of God.

15:16   I am chosen and appointed by Christ to bear His _____.

Romans 8:1   I am free forever from _____.

8:17   I am a joint _____ with Christ, sharing His inheritance with Him.

1 Corinthians 6:17   I am _____ with the Lord and am one spirit with Him.

6:19, 20   I have been _____ with a price; I am not my own; I belong to God.

2 Corinthians 5:17   I am a new _____.

5:21   I have been made _____.

Galatians 2:20   Christ lives in _____. The life I am now living is Christ's life.

Ephesians 1:3   I have been blessed with every _____ blessing.

1:4   I was chosen in Christ before the foundation of the world to be _____, and I am without blame before Him.

Colossians 2:7   I am firmly _____ in Christ and am now being built up in Him.

2:10   I have been made _____ in Christ.

2 Timothy 1:7 I have been given a Spirit of _____, love, and self-discipline.

Hebrews 4:16 I have the right to come boldly before the throne of God to receive

_____ and find grace to help in time of need.

2 Peter 1:4 I have been given precious and magnificent promises by God,

by which I am a partaker of God's _____ nature.

1 John 5:18 I am born of _____, and the evil one cannot touch me.

(The above study has been adapted from *Victory Over the Darkness*, by Neil T. Anderson, Regal Books, 1990.)

MEDITATING ON GOD'S VIEW OF YOU

For the next two weeks, read the above list out loud every day. Think about what it means to be a child of God. When you are tempted to sin, remember that you have God's mighty power working in you.

Use Paul's words below to ask God to change you from the inside:

Now to Him who is able to do above and beyond all that we ask or think–according to the power that works in you–to Him be glory in the church and in Christ Jesus to all generations, forever and ever. Amen. (**Ephesians 3:20-21**)

DAY 4 SUMMARY

Describe your spiritual birthright as a child of the King:

_____

_____

EXPLORING THE WORLD OF IDEAS

If you have not checked the papers this week for articles dealing with worldview topics, take a few minutes to do it now.

WEEK 5, DAY 5
TOTAL COMMITMENT

THE CHICKEN, THE COW AND TOTAL COMMITMENT

A chicken and a cow were walking together when they passed a restaurant with a sign in the window: "Breakfast Special: Steak and eggs, $7.50." The chicken suggested that they both go in for a meal. The cow replied, "For you, that's just a contribution. But for me, it means total commitment!"

Okay, so it's only a semi-funny joke. But it makes a point. If the chicken and cow represent two different attitudes towards being a Christian, how would you describe each one?

The chicken is like a Christian who . . .

_____

_____

The cow represents a follower of Christ who . . .

_____

_____

You probably know some friends who are like the chicken in the above story—willing to make a "contribution" to the cause of Christ, spend a little time at church, basically be a "nice" person, not murder anybody, stay out of trouble with the law—but the "total commitment" thing? You've got to be kidding!

LIVING LIKE A PIG

Living on the fringe of the Christian life can also be compared to another farm animal, namely a pig! In *How To Be Your Own Selfish Pig*, Susan Schaeffer Macaulay explains how to become a selfish pig by using the following morning routine:

Get up early enough to spend several hours on your personal appearance. . . . look in the mirror and practice several key lines: "I gotta be me." "This doesn't meet my needs right now." "Hey, give me a little space!" "I can't help it; that's just the way I am." . . . As you walk [out the door], make a mental list of whom to say hello to and whom to ignore. . . . If you're ever at a loss for words to express your superiority over other human beings, simply apply the tip of your index finger to the tip of your nose and push upward gently.[4]

Of course, people are free to live as selfish pigs if they choose. But the principles in the following verses should be a warning about the consequences of that type of self-centered pursuit. Read each passage and answer the questions:

Hebrews 10:26-31

(1) What terms used in this passage tells you this is written to Christians? _____

_____

(2) If a Christian keeps on sinning deliberately, what can he expect from God? _____

_____

(3) What might some of those judgments be?

_____

_____

(4) Complete the verse: "It is a _____ thing to fall into the hands of the _____ God."

Proverbs 3:11-12

(1) As a child of God, you are called His _____.

(2) The writer uses the analogy of a father and son. In what two ways does the father relate to his son?

_____

_____

3) Because a father loves his son, he _____ his son.

Hebrews 10:26-31

For if we deliberately sin after receiving the knowledge of the truth, there no longer remains a sacrifice for sins, [27]but a terrifying expectation of judgment, and the fury of a fire about to consume the adversaries. [28]If anyone disregards Moses' law, he dies without mercy, based on the testimony of two or three witnesses. [29]How much worse punishment, do you think one will deserve who has trampled on the Son of God, regarded as profane the blood of the covenant by which he was sanctified, and insulted the Spirit of grace? [30]For we know the One who has said, "Vengeance belongs to Me, I will repay," and again, "The Lord will judge His people." [31]It is a terrifying thing to fall into the hands of the living God!

Proverbs 3:11-12

*Do not despise the LORD's instruction, my son, and do not loathe His discipline;
[12]for the LORD disciplines the one He loves, just as a father, the son he delights in.*

God, as our Heavenly Father, loves us enough to discipline us when we live selfishly. This should cause us to respond in what way? (Choose one—there is a right answer!)

❐   By being angry with God for His discipline and staying away from Him.

❐   By not "losing heart" and being encouraged that God cares.

❐   By having a "don't care" attitude and being discouraged.

PICK YOUR BARNYARD PERSONALITY

Honestly, as it relates to your Christian life, which barnyard animal are you more like?
(check your answer)

❐   The chicken – willing to contribute a little.

❐   The pig – thinking mostly of yourself.

❐   The cow – totally committed to Jesus.

If you checked "A" or "B," the more important question for you is: which one would you like to be? In light of the ultimate sacrifice that Jesus made for you, is there any good reason to live a "chicken" or "pig" type of Christian life? _____

POSITIVE PSYCHOLOGICAL HEALTH!

Schaeffer outlines a simple approach to "positive psychological hygiene": "As a Christian, instead of putting myself in practice at the center of the universe, I must do something else. This is not only right, and the failure to do so is not only sin, but it is important for me personally in this life. I must think after God, and I must will after God."
(TLAC, 76)

List some practical ways that you can think and will after God:

(1) _____

(2) _____

(3) _____

DAY 5 SUMMARY:

What are two things you can do to move toward a more total commitment to Christ?

(1)_____

(2)_____

WEEK 5 SUMMARY: PSYCHOLOGY

Biblical Christian psychology deals with the total "you": body and soul. By your trusting Jesus as your Savior, God accepts you as His child. Positive self-esteem is a result of replacing your negative thoughts about yourself with God's perspective. By continuing to focus on God's view of you, you will be motivated to submit to the Lordship of Christ and live a life that is pleasing to Him.

REVIEW KEY VERSE

Colossians 2:13   *And when you were dead in trespasses and in the uncircumcision of your flesh, He made you _____ with Him and forgave us all our trespasses.*

ENDNOTES
1. Susan Schaeffer Macaulay, *How To Be Your Own Selfish Pig* (Zondervan Publishing House, 1982), pp. 84-5.
2. Ibid, p. 85.
3. Ibid, p. 87.
4. Ibid, pp. 106-7.

SCRIPTURE SUPPLEMENT

John 1:12 *But to all who did receive Him He gave them the right to be children of God, to those who believe in His name*

15:16 *You did not choose Me, but I chose you. I appointed you that you should go out and produce fruit, and that your fruit should remain, so that whatever you ask the Father in My name, He will give you.*

Romans 8:1 *Therefore, no condemnation now exists for those in Christ Jesus.*

8:17 *and if children, also heirs—heirs of God and co-heirs with Christ—seeing that we suffer with Him so that we may also be glorified with Him.*

1 Corinthians 6:17, 19-20 *But anyone joined to the Lord is one spirit with Him. . . . ⁱ⁹Do you not know that your body is a sanctuary of the Holy Spirit who is in you, whom you have from God? You are not your own, ²⁰for you were bought at a price; therefore glorify God in your body.*

2 Corinthians 5:17 *Therefore if anyone is in Christ, there is a new creation; old things have passed away, and look, new things have come.*

5:21 *He made the One who did not know sin to be sin for us, so that we might become the righteousness of God in Him.*

Galatians 2:20 *and I no longer live, but Christ lives in me. The life I now live in the flesh, I live by faith in the Son of God, who loved me and gave Himself for me.*

Ephesians 1:3-4 *Blessed be the God and Father of our Lord Jesus Christ, who has blessed us with every spiritual blessing in the heavens, in Christ; ⁴for He chose us in Him, before the foundation of the world, to be holy and blameless in His sight.*

Colossians 2:7 *rooted and built up in Him and established in the faith, just as you were taught, and overflowing with thankfulness.*

2:10 *and you have been filled by Him, who is the head over every ruler and authority.*

2 Timothy 1:7 *For God has not given us a spirit of fearfulness, but one of power, love, and sound judgment.*

Hebrews 4:16 *Therefore let us approach the throne of grace with boldness, so that we may receive mercy and find grace to help us at the proper time.*

2 Peter 1:4 *By these He has given us very great and precious promises, so that through them you may share in the divine nature, escaping the corruption that is in the world because of evil desires.*

1 John 5:18 *We know that everyone who has been born of God does not sin, but the One who is born of God keeps him, and the evil one does not touch him.*

WEEK 6: ETHICS

IS THERE ANY REAL RIGHT OR WRONG?

"Of course there is 'right' and 'wrong,'" you may be saying. You were probably brought up to know that certain things are right to do and other things are wrong. But have you ever stopped to think about where these ideas of right and wrong come from?

Some people believe that society decides what is acceptable behavior, with some cultures developing different moral standards from others. If this is true, then morality is whatever you have been raised to believe. But are your culture's ideas true for someone living in a different culture halfway around the globe? Or how about someone living five hundred years ago? Or five hundred years in the future? Maybe five hundred years from now people will have a different moral code. And even in our culture, who's to say what is the right thing to do, anyway? It all depends on the situation, right? . . . or is that wrong?

This week, you will find out:

▼ "Who says" what is right and what is wrong

▼ What an "absolute" is and how mankind has distorted God's moral standards

▼ The greatest way you can please God and how to put that into your daily experience

▼ If feeling "guilty" is good

▼ How to maintain a close relationship with the God of the universe!

WEEK 6, DAY 1

THE GRAND "SAYS WHO?"

FIRST, A LITTLE TEST

Circle the word that you feel best completes the sentence according to your ethical worldview:

▼ Drinking and driving is (irresponsible / responsible).

▼ Pushing a little child down a staircase is (perverse / life-enhancing).

▼ Taking your share of the chores is (evil / good).

▼ Poking a sharp stick in another person's eye is (revolting / entertaining).

Why did you circle the words you did?

_____

It may seem obvious that some behavior is right and other actions wrong. It just makes sense not to drink and drive, and it seems revolting to poke a stick in someone's eye. But why are these things wrong? Where do these ideas of "right and wrong" come from?

Where did you get *your* ideas about ethics?

_____

Here is an issue you must consider: In our society there are many conflicting views about what is right or wrong. When different sources suggest contrary moral values, how do you decide which ones to follow? Or, in other words, "Who says" that this is right and that is wrong?

THE IDEA OF MORAL LAW

Christian writer and philosopher C. S. Lewis says it this way:

> *Think of a country where people were admired for running away from battle, or where a man felt proud of double-crossing all the people who had been kindest to him. You*

might just as well try to imagine a country where two and two make five. . . . Men have differed as to whether you should have one wife or four. But they have always agreed that you must not simply have any woman you liked.[1]

Citing the International Values Survey, English sociologist David Martin concludes, "we are mostly agreed about good and bad. People are, it seems, adamantly opposed to lying, stealing, cheating, coveting, killing, and dishonoring their parents."[2]

Based on these two quotations, what can you conclude concerning the origin of ethics?

_____

_____

ETHICS AND THEOLOGY

Christian ethics is inseparable from theology because Christian ethics is grounded in the character of God. "One of the distinctions of the Judeo-Christian God," says Francis Schaeffer, "is that not all things are the same to Him. That at first may sound rather trivial, but in reality it is one of the most profound things one can say about the Judeo-Christian God. He exists; He has a character; and not all things are the same to Him. Some things conform to His character, and some are opposed to His character." The task of Christian ethics is determining what conforms to God's character and what does not. (TLAC, 81)

According to Schaeffer, what is one of the most profound things about biblical Christianity?

_____

_____

A unique aspect of a biblical worldview is that ethics is tied into the _____ of God. So to the question, "Who says what is right and wrong?", the answer is,

"God says, that's who!"

Since ethics have their source, or origin, in God's character, what do we need to do to determine what is right and wrong?

_____

_____

Psalm 96:9-13

Worship the LORD in His holy majesty; tremble before Him, all the earth.
¹⁰Say among the nations: "The LORD reigns. The world is firmly established; it cannot be shaken. He judges the peoples fairly."
¹¹Let the heavens be glad and the earth rejoice; let the sea and all that fills it resound.
¹²Let the fields and everything in them exult. Then all the trees of the forest will shout for joy before the LORD for He is coming— for
¹³He is coming to judge the earth. He will judge the world with righteousness and the peoples with His faithfulness.

Which of the three characteristics of God noted in Week 2, Day 3 relates most closely to our discussion of "ethics"?

_____

_____

GOD'S CHARACTER AND YOU

Spend a few minutes reflecting on the holiness of God. Read **Psalm 96:9-13**. Based on this psalm, write your thoughts concerning God's holiness and your behavior.

_____

_____

_____

DAY 1 SUMMARY

How does God's righteousness provide a foundation for ethics?

_____

_____

_____

WEEK 6 KEY VERSE

Colossians 3:17 *And whatever you do, in word or in deed, do everything in the name of the Lord Jesus, giving thanks to God the Father through him.*

WEEK 6, DAY 2

MORAL ABSOLUTES? ABSOLUTELY!

IT ALL DEPENDS!

You've probably heard it said: "What's right for you might not be right for someone else. Everything depends on the situation."

What do you think of those statements? Write a short critique.

_____

_____

If everything is "relative," that would mean there are no "absolute" standards of right and wrong. However, the biblical Christian worldview claims to provide an ethical standard by which to gauge what is right. See if you can follow the logic of this next statement as you fill in the appropriate worldview categories. (Use our terms theology, philosophy, biology, psychology, or ethics.)

If . . . God is real (as we learned in our study of P_____),

and God's character is righteous (from our study of T_____),

and God designed life to work in a certain way (our study of B_____),

and God made man to reflect His character (from biblical P_____),

then . . . it follows that there are absolute standards of conduct

that are true for all people, in all situations, and throughout all time,

(as we are discovering in our current study of E_____).

Do you see the connection between all the worldview categories we've studied so far?

WHAT IS AN "ABSOLUTE"?

When we talk about an absolute standard, we mean a standard that does not change for any reason. Think about a ruler or tape measure. An inch is the same no matter where you live or in what circumstances you may find yourself.

Genesis 2:22-24

Then the LORD God built the rib He had taken from the man into a woman and brought her to the man. 23 And the man said, This one at last is bone of my bone, and flesh of my flesh; this one will be called woman, for this one was taken from man.
24 This is why a man leaves his father and his mother and bonds with his wife and they become one flesh.

Proverbs 12:22

Lying lips are detestable to the LORD, but those who act faithfully are His delight.

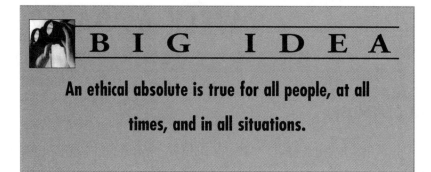

BIG IDEA

An ethical absolute is true for all people, at all times, and in all situations.

In the same way, God has established absolute standards that do not change with location, situation, culture, or time.

Biblical Christianity champions the concept of ethical absolutes. But what specific absolutes make up the moral order? Make a list of a few:

_____   _____

_____   _____

_____   _____

THE ABSOLUTE NATURE OF ETHICAL ABSOLUTES

Absolutes are revealed in the Bible. While it is impossible for every specific situation requiring moral decisions to be included in the Bible, the Christian is given enough specific values and guidelines to have a sense of what is right and what is wrong in all situations. The most obvious absolutes, of course, are the Ten Commandments—the Decalogue. This acts as the "basic law" for mankind, but it is not the only law revealed in the Bible. Much of the Old Testament is dedicated to describing God's moral order. (TLAC, 84-5)

The Bible is not one long list of "do's and don'ts" that cover every aspect of your life. God created you with the freedom to make moral choices. This means that, in the Scriptures, God's commands and His general principles form a moral framework from which we all make ethical decisions.

IDEAS HAVE CONSEQUENCES

Each of these passages describes the way that God designed human relationships to work best. In the chart below, summarize God's moral plan. Then, write the ways that people have distorted it due to their sin, and in the last column, list some of the consequences of trying to live outside of God's moral framework.

GOD'S MORAL PLAN

	MAN'S DISTORTION	NEGATIVE CONSEQUENCES
Genesis 2:22-24		
Proverbs 12:22		
Matthew 6:25-27		
1 Corinthians 6:18-20		

If we follow man's distorted ideas about God's moral design, there are significant and negative consequences to those actions. On the other hand, what would the world be like if everyone, in every place, always practiced the following general principles?

GOD'S MORAL PLAN

Positive Consequences

Genesis 2:22-24	A family consists of a man and a woman loving each other for life.
Proverbs 12:22	Tell the truth.
Matthew 6:25-27	Trust God for the future.
1 Corinthians 6:18-20	Reserve sexual intimacy for marriage.

MORALITY IN THE REAL WORLD

Look for examples of how ideas have consequences. Check the newspaper or a weekly news magazine for articles that illustrate people's moral choices. Bring these to your next group session or private lesson.

Matthew 6:25-27

This is why I tell you: Don't worry about your life, what you will eat or what you will drink; or about your body, what you will wear. Isn't life more than food and the body more than clothing? [26]Look at the birds of the sky: they don't sow or reap or gather into barns, yet your heavenly Father feeds them. Aren't you worth more than they? [27]Can any of you add a single cubit to his height by worrying?

1 Corinthians 6:18-20

Flee from sexual immorality! "Every sin a person can commit is outside the body," but the person who is sexually immoral sins against his own body. [19]Do you not know that your body is a sanctuary of the Holy Spirit who is in you, whom you have from God? You are not your own, [20]for you were bought at a price; therefore glorify God in your body.

DAY 2 SUMMARY

Who's to say what is right and wrong? And why?

_____

_____

DIGGING DEEPER: *Moral relativism is the predominant view in our society. Using the following quotation, identify the worldview categories that are implicated by the statement (there are at least five) and the underlying assumptions associated with each category. Then, based on Provine's worldview, evaluate how he might respond to current ethical issues such as abortion, human cloning, or gay marriage.*

> "No inherent moral or ethical laws exist, nor are there absolute guiding principles for human society. The universe cares nothing for us and we have no ultimate meaning in life." -- William Provine *(quoted in* Understanding the Times, *David A. Noebel, Harvest House Publishers, 1991, p. 193.)*

For more practical ideas on how to defend absolute truth and morality, see Relativism: Feet Firmly Planted in Mid-Air, *by Frank Beckwith and Greg Koukl. The book, along with a video interview of the authors and a leader's guide for six group lessons may be ordered online through Summit Ministries at www.summit.org and by clicking on "Curriculum."*

WEEK 6, DAY 3

LOVING GOD, LOVING OTHERS

THE GREATEST

If you had to pick one ethical law as the most important to follow, what would you choose?

The greatest ethical law is _____

_____

Jesus had some things to say about the greatest of God's standards. Read **Mark 12:28-31**, and write in your own words the most important ethical principle according to Jesus.

_____

_____

What does it mean to love God with all your heart?

_____

. . .with all your soul?

_____

. . .with all your mind?

_____

. . .with all your strength?

_____

IF YOU WANT TO BE HAPPY. . .

"The moral end, or highest good, is the glory of God," writes William Young. *"In declaring by word and deed the perfections, especially the moral perfections of the most High, man finds true happiness."* (TLAC, 87)

Mark 12:28-31

One of the scribes approached. When he heard them debating and saw that Jesus answered them well he asked Him, "Which commandment is the most important of all?" [29]*"This is the most important," Jesus answered: "Hear, O Israel! The Lord our God is one Lord.* [30]*And you shall love the Lord your God with all your heart, with all your soul, with all your mind, and with all your strength.'* [31]*The second is: 'You shall love your neighbor as yourself.' There is no other commandment greater than these."*

Luke 10:29-37

But wanting to justify himself, he asked Jesus, "And who is my neighbor?"

³⁰Jesus took up the question and said: "A man was going down from Jerusalem to Jericho and fell into the hands of robbers. They stripped him, beat him up, and fled, leaving him half dead. ³¹A priest happened to be going down that road. When he saw him, he passed by on the other side. ³²In the same way, a Levite, when he arrived at the place and saw him, passed by on the other side. ³³But a Samaritan, while traveling, came up to him; and when he saw the man, he had compassion. ³⁴He went over to him and bandaged his wounds, pouring on oil and wine. Then he put him on his own animal, brought him to an inn, and took care of him. ³⁵The next day he took out two denarii, gave them to the innkeeper, and said, 'Take care of him; and when I come back I'll reimburse you for whatever extra you spend.' ³⁶Which of these three do you think proved to be a neighbor to the man who fell into the hands of the robbers?"

³⁷"The one who showed mercy to him," he said. Then Jesus told him, "Go and do the same."

The above quote points out how to find true happiness. What is it?

_____

Can you list some of "God's perfections"?

_____

How could you "declare by word" the perfections of God?

_____

_____

> *This duty toward our fellow man requires more than serving his spiritual needs. "[M]an is more than a soul destined for another world," says Norman Geisler, "he is also a body living in this world. And as a resident of this time-space continuum man has physical and social needs which cannot be isolated from spiritual needs. Hence, in order to love man as he is—the whole man—one must exercise a concern about his social needs as well as his spiritual needs."*
> (TLAC, 86)

In what ways could you "declare by deed" the perfections of God?

_____

_____

LOVING GOD BY LOVING OTHERS

In Mark 12, Jesus also points to a second commandment: That our love for God should overflow into love for our fellow man. If we truly love God, one way we can demonstrate that love is through _____ our fellow man.

> *The love of God is the service of man in love.*
> (TLAC, 86)

MEETING REAL NEEDS

According to Jesus' story about the Good Samaritan in Luke 10:29-37, a "neighbor" is defined as anyone you know who has a need.

Whom do you know that qualifies as your "neighbor," and what is that person's physical need?

_____

_____

How could you demonstrate God's love by helping meet that need?

_____

PUTTING LOVE INTO PRACTICE

Why not put into practice what you are learning about loving God and loving others? You may want to sing a praise chorus that describes the majesty of God. Singing reminds you about God's moral character and helps to imprint those thoughts in your mind.

Then, in quiet reflection, ask God how you can "declare His perfections" in deed. As He brings people and thoughts to your mind, write down specific ways that you can demonstrate love toward a "neighbor."

(1) _____

(2) _____

(3) _____

DAY 3 SUMMARY

What will lead you to true happiness?

_____

_____

REVIEW KEY VERSE

Colossians 3:17 *And whatever you do, in _____ or in _____, do everything in the name of the Lord Jesus, giving thanks to God the Father through Him.*

WEEK 6, DAY 4

THE ULTIMATE GUILT TRIP

Romans 1:16-19

For I am not ashamed of the gospel, because it is God's power for salvation to everyone who believes, first to the Jew, and also to the Greek. [17]For in it God's righteousness is revealed from faith to faith, just as it is written: "The righteous will live by faith."

[18]For God's wrath is revealed from heaven against all godlessness and unrighteousness of people who by their unrighteousness suppress the truth, [19]since what can be known about God is evident among them, because God has shown it to them.

THE MORAL ATMOSPHERE

In today's society, it's becoming increasingly difficult to follow God's ethical standards. Our whole culture is moving quickly away from a moral orientation to one of "do your own thing." It's as if we are living under a giant hole in the "moral ozone."

According to a survey of nearly 7,000 high school and college students. . .

▼ One third of the high school students said that they had taken an item from a store without paying for it within the previous year.

▼ 60% had lied to their parents.

▼ Honesty ranked lower in their priorities than getting into college and securing a well-paying job.[3]

Lying, stealing and dishonesty relate to some pretty basic moral ideas. As this kind of behavior becomes more widespread, what would you expect to happen to our society?

_____

EVERYONE BEHAVING BADLY

Maybe somebody should produce a movie called *Everyone Behaving Badly.* Have you noticed anyone behaving badly in your community? In what ways? Make a short list:

(1) _____ (4) _____

(2) _____ (5) _____

(3) _____ (6) _____

Why do you think people act this way? _____
_____

Read **Romans 1:16-19** for a further answer to the above question. It seems that people everywhere are aware of God's moral laws, but they refuse to obey them. Why?

_____

Have you ever tried to talk to someone about sin? Try bringing up the word "sin" in a conversation with your friends, and see what happens! You'll probably hear:

"Don't start preaching to me about sin! You can't put that guilt trip on me."

How would you respond to that kind of comment? _____

_____

THE "GUILT" ALARM

This conviction of guilt is crucial for a Christian to understand the incredible sacrifice God made when He sent His Son to die for us. The Christian ethical code calls for perfection, and no one other than Christ has ever achieved that. Thus, it is the ethical code itself that points man first to his own sinful nature and then to the realization that the only One who can save him is the Man who has not stepped outside the moral code, Jesus Christ. The absolute moral code shows us our absolute dependence on Him. (TLAC, 88)

To help you get a handle on "guilt," think about an alarm clock. What is its purpose? It alerts you when it's time to wake up. You may not like the alarm clock waking you from a sound sleep, but you don't blame it for doing what it is supposed to do!

Guilt is like an alarm clock. Feelings of guilt are a "wake-up call" to alert you to your need to turn from that sinful behavior and ask for God's forgiveness.

Why should you talk to your friends about their failure to meet God's moral standards?

_____

A SPIRITUAL CROWBAR

The next time you are talking with your non-Christian friends, go ahead and talk about "sin," but don't use it as a hammer to pound them about their sinful behavior. Use it as a crowbar to open up their understanding of God's moral universe and its implications for their lives.

Revelation 22:16-17

"I, Jesus, have sent My angel to attest these things to you for the churches. I am the Root and the Offspring of David, the Bright Morning Star."

[17]Both the Spirit and the bride say, "Come!" Anyone who hears should say, "Come!" And the one who is thirsty should come. Whoever desires should take the living water as a gift.

MAKING IT HAPPEN WHERE YOU LIVE

When Jesus stepped out of eternity into time, He provided the solution to our sin problem. Consider **Revelation 22:16-17**, and write the verses in your own words.

_____

_____

_____

 PRAY ABOUT IT!

Pray for your friends who need to understand their sin problem and the solution found in Jesus Christ. How can you, in a tactful way, help them understand the real reason that people behave badly?

_____

DAY 4 SUMMARY

What should guilt alert you to, and why is that good?

_____

EXPLORING OUR CULTURAL OZONE HOLE

Cut out an article or two from your local newspaper that reflect the moral "ozone hole" we are experiencing.

FOR GROUP STUDY: Be ready to discuss these from a biblical worldview when you bring them to the next lesson.

FOR INDIVIDUAL STUDY: Write a short paragraph that describes the moral ozone hole you see in the article(s).

WEEK 6, DAY 5

PERSONAL MORAL INVENTORY

JUST DON'T TALK ABOUT. . .

Look at **Revelation 21:8**. What is the destination for people who disobey God's moral law? _____

A fiery lake of burning sulfur is not a very appealing picture. From this passage and others, the Bible speaks of a time in the future when God will judge non-Christians for their conduct.

But someone might say, "Don't talk about that 'fire and brimstone' stuff. What are you trying to do, scare people into becoming a Christian?"

So, what's your opinion? Should you tell people about...you know...the other place...(Hell)? What do you think?

❑ Yes, tell them about "Hell."

❑ No, fear is not a good motivator.

❑ I'm not sure, convince me!

MOTIVATED BY FEAR?

Is fear a good motivator? To answer that question, think about this: Why do you warn a little child not to play in the street or touch a hot stove?

_____

Of course, either fear or love can motivate people. That's why the gospel is like the two sides of a coin. When we share the "good news," obviously, we are referring to God's love and forgiveness. But unless people also understand that God will judge sin—which is the "bad news"—they may not be motivated to respond to God's love.

> ## Revelation 21:8
>
> "*But the cowards, unbelievers, vile, murderers, sexually immoral, sorcerers, idolaters, and all liars–their share will be in the lake that burns with fire and sulfur, which is the second death.*

2 PETER 3:9-14

The Lord does not delay His promise, as some understand delay, but is patient with you, not wanting any to perish, but all to come to repentance. ¹⁰But the day of the Lord will come like a thief; on that day the heavens will pass away with a loud noise, the elements will burn and be dissolved, and the earth and the works on it will be disclosed. ¹¹Since all these things are to be destroyed in this way, it is clear what sort of people you should be in holy conduct and godliness ¹²as you wait for and earnestly desire the coming of the day of God, because of which the heavens will be on fire and be dissolved, and the elements will melt with the heat. ¹³But based on His promise, we wait for new heavens and a new earth, where righteousness will dwell. ¹⁴Therefore, dear friends, while you wait for these things, make every effort to be found in peace without spot or blemish before Him.

We shouldn't dismiss either side of the gospel "coin" as we try to help our friends and neighbors understand their need to accept Christ as Savior and Lord.

Paul says the same thing in **2 Corinthians 5:10-11**:

> *For we must all appear before the judgment seat of Christ, so that each may be repaid for what he has done in the body, whether good or bad. ¹¹Knowing, then, the fear of the Lord, we persuade people. . .*

WHAT'S THE CONNECTION?

What does all this talk about sin and punishment have to do with ethics? Plenty! First of all, it points out the fact that God takes sin seriously. And if He takes the sins of non-Christians seriously, He also takes the sins of Christians seriously.

Read **2 Peter 3:9-14**. The subject concerns God's future judgment of the entire earth. In light of God's judgment, how should you be living today?

_____

_____

See **Luke 7:36-50** in the "Scripture Supplement" section on pages 105-6.

Once you see the magnitude of your sin problem, you will also see the magnitude of God's love. Jesus said the same thing in Luke 7:36-50. What is the point Jesus makes in this passage?

_____

_____

STAYING IN A RIGHT RELATIONSHIP WITH GOD

> *The Christian cannot, however, simply rely on Christ to save him, and then continue in his sinful ways. Rather, once the Christian understands the*

ultimate sacrifice God made for him, he cannot help but respond with a grateful desire to please God by adhering to His moral order. (TLAC, 88)

Even though you may have become His child by trusting Jesus for your sins, you still disobey His moral commands at times. God takes this disobedience seriously, and it breaks your fellowship with Him.

Fortunately, there is a way to restore fellowship with God once we realize we have sinned. The process is based on **1 John 1:9**:

> *If we confess our sins, He is faithful and righteous to forgive us our sins and cleanse us from all unrighteousness.*

This verse offers some principles that allow you to maintain a close walk with God.

THE "ABC'S" OF WALKING WITH GOD

The *"A"* stands for *"Agree"* with God about your sin. Don't try to make excuses for what you have done. God wants you to simply admit that you were wrong—that's what "confession" means.

Are you aware of any areas in your life that you need to confess to God? If so, do it now.

The *"B"* stands for *"Believe"* God's promise. 1 John 1:9 states that God will cleanse you of your unrighteous behavior. Did you notice that God's forgiveness is linked to His character? What two aspects of God's character form the basis for His forgiveness?

(1) _____

(2) _____

God is right to forgive you because Jesus paid the penalty for your sin. God took the punishment that you deserve and placed it on Jesus when He died on the cross. In that way, God's justice has been met.

> If you confessed your sin(s) to God, do you now believe that He has forgiven you of all your sins?
>
> _____
>
> If so, thank Him for His unconditional love and forgiveness to experience His complete cleansing.
>
> _____

> ## Ephesians 5:18-21
>
> *And don't get drunk with wine, which leads to reckless actions, but be filled with the Spirit:* *[19]speaking to one another in psalms, hymns, and spiritual songs, singing and making music to the Lord in your heart, [20]giving thanks always for everything to God the Father in the name of our Lord Jesus Christ, [21]submitting to one another in the fear of Christ.*

The *"C"* stands for *"Control."* This means that you want to allow Jesus Christ to direct your life—every part of it. Look at **Ephesians 5:18**. This verse says that there is something you should not do and something else that you should do.

What should you *not do*? _____

What should you *do*? _____

Being "filled" with the Spirit means allowing the Holy Spirit to influence and direct your life. Colossians 3:16 suggests something else that should fill your life. What is that?

_____
_____
_____

Now notice the similarity of results as you compare Ephesians 5:18-21 with Colossians 3:16-17. Are these the characteristics you want to be true about you? Write a prayer that focuses on your desire to allow Christ's Spirit and His Word to fill each area of your life.

_____
_____
_____

DAY 5 SUMMARY

Review 1 John 1:9 and fill in the blanks below:

If we _____ our sins, He is _____and righteous to _____ us our sins and cleanse us from all unrighteousness.

What happens when people sin, and what hope do we have for recovery?

_____

WEEK 6 SUMMARY: ETHICS

Our culture screams that morality doesn't matter. Yet, all of human history declares two important truths:

> #1 - *Everybody understands there are certain moral standards, and*
>
> #2 - *Everybody breaks those standards.*

That is why only the biblical Christian worldview makes any sense. Because there is a God who is holy and righteous, each person can seek God's forgiveness for disobeying His moral code. Only then can we experience true inner peace and begin the journey into living for God according to His moral law.

REVIEW KEY VERSE

Colossians 3:17 *And whatever you do, in word or in deed, do everything in the name of the Lord Jesus, _____ _____ to God the Father through him.*

ENDNOTES

1. Quoted in "Not So Christian America," Thomas C. Reeves, *First Things*, October 1996, p.18.

2. Ibid.

3. "Honesty May No Longer be the Best Policy," Richard Morin, *Washington Post Weekly*, Dec. 7, 1997, p.36.

SCRIPTURE SUPPLEMENT

Luke 7:36-50 *Then one of the Pharisees invited Him to eat with him. He entered the Pharisee's house and reclined at the table. [37]And a woman in the town who was a sinner found out that Jesus was reclining at the table in the Pharisee's house. She brought an alabaster flask of fragrant oil [38]and stood behind Him at His feet, weeping, and began to wash His feet with her tears. She wiped His feet with the hair of her head, kissing them and anointing them with the fragrant oil.*

[39]When the Pharisee who had invited Him saw this, he said to himself, "This man, if He were a prophet, would know who and what kind of woman this is who is touching Him—that she's a sinner!"

Colossians 3:16-17

Let the message about the Messiah dwell richly among you, teaching and admonishing one another in all wisdom, and singing psalms, hymns, and spiritual songs, with gratitude in your hearts to God. [17]And whatever you do, in word or in deed, do everything in the name of the Lord Jesus, giving thanks to God the Father through Him.

⁴⁰Jesus replied to him, "Simon, I have something to say to you."

"Teacher," he said, "say it."

⁴¹"A creditor had two debtors. One owed five hundred denarii, and the other fifty. ⁴²Since they could not pay it back, he graciously forgave them both. So, which of them will love him more?"

⁴³Simon answered, "I suppose the one he forgave more."

"You have judged correctly," He told him. ⁴⁴Turning to the woman, He said to Simon, "Do you see this woman? I entered your house; you gave Me no water for My feet, but she, with her tears, has washed My feet and wiped them with her hair. ⁴⁵You gave Me no kiss, but she hasn't stopped kissing My feet since I came in. ⁴⁶You didn't anoint My head with oil, but she has anointed My feet with fragrant oil. ⁴⁷Therefore I tell you, her many sins have been forgiven; that's why she loved much. But the one who is forgiven little, loves little." ⁴⁸Then He said to her, "Your sins are forgiven."

⁴⁹Those who were at the table with Him began to say among themselves, "Who is this man who even forgives sins?"

⁵⁰And He said to the woman, "Your faith has saved you. Go in peace."

WEEK 7: SOCIOLOGY

WHAT MAKES A HEALTHY SOCIETY?

Have you ever noticed how few hermits there are in the world? Most folks just naturally want to be around other people.

Sociology deals with this issue of living together in society. As a part of an overall worldview, it asks the question: What is the basis for a healthy society? According to the Bible, there are at least three ways people live together—the family, the church, and the state.

Living in a healthy society sounds good, but we quickly realize that each level of society has its own benefits and pitfalls. The family can be a place of great love and blessing or one of fear and abuse. Churches can fulfill their role of spreading the gospel and serving those in need or fall apart into factions. The state can be the means to unify people to protect God-given rights of life and liberty, or it can become a bureaucracy that imposes high taxes and takes away freedom from the people.

This week you will explore God's design for society. You will discover that His plan for the family and the church provides the very best way to develop as individuals and to get along with other people. The institution of the state will be discussed more fully under the topic of "politics" in a couple of weeks.

This week, you can expect to learn about:

▼ What it means to be a social creature

▼ The vital signs of a healthy society

▼ How to change our society for the better

▼ Why families are the bedrock of all societies

▼ The importance of the church for maintaining a civilized culture

So share with your family the things that you learn this week. You'll be glad you did, and so will they!

WEEK 7, DAY 1

YOU'RE A WHAT?

"Chris," says Skip, "If this statement applied to you, how would you fill in the blank: I am a _____ animal?"

Chris thought a minute and said, "Party, as in 'party animal?'"

"I don't think so," replied Skip. "That may describe me, but definitely not you."

"Okay. How about 'intelligent'?"

"A strong 'maybe.' But even though you were in the top ten percent of our graduating class, you're a little slim on common sense," came the rebuttal from Skip. "I know, you are a featherless bi-pedal animal! But then again, so is a plucked chicken!"

Skip let out a loud cackle as he walked away, leaving Chris wondering why he had brought up the subject in the first place.

What are some other possible ways to complete Skip's statement? Chris might have said he was a social animal. What do you think about that answer? Does it fit you, too?

If we are serious, we all would admit that deep down, we are social creatures. But why is that the case? Complete the following sentence:

We are social creatures because _____

_____

BACK TO THE PAST

It seems that we can't get away from going back to our biblical theology to answer questions that come from other categories, like this question that deals with sociology. Take a look at **Genesis 1** and **2** in the Scripture Supplement on pages 125-7, and answer the following questions:

In chapter one, we are told that God liked all that He created. Scan the chapter for the phrase that describes His creation (see verses 10, 12, 18, 21, 25, 31):

"God saw that it was _____."

In Genesis 2 we are introduced to some details that are not included in the overview of creation in Chapter 1. What is one of the first things God said after creating Adam (see 2:18)?

"It is _____ good for the man to be _____."

God knew something about the man He had just created: Adam was not made to be alone. After stating that there was no helper suitable for Adam, God created _____ (read 2:19-20).

Do you find it interesting that God brought all those animals to Adam? Why do you think He did that? _____

_____

_____

In naming the animals, apparently God was giving Adam an object lesson from nature. As Adam studied and named all the animals, he must have recognized that there were male and female counterparts. Yet, as he looked around, he began to realize that there was no counterpart for him! No suitable helper was found.

Adam must have experienced loneliness.

You know what happens next. Review Genesis 2:21-23, and notice Adam's comment when he first sees Eve. An English translation doesn't convey the original language as well, but Adam's response is more of a . . .

"WOW, FINALLY SOMEONE LIKE ME!"

Was he excited, or what? If you had been Adam, you would have been excited, too. Finally, the writer gives us a general principle based on the account of Adam and Eve. Look at verse 24.

"For this reason a man will _____ his father and mother and be _____ to his wife, and they will become _____ flesh."

> *S.D. Gaede stresses the inherent social nature of man, stating, "God designed the human being to be a relational creature. Note this point well. Humankind was created to relate to other beings. It was not an accident. It was not the result of sin. It was an intentional, creational given."* (TLAC, 96)

Relating to other people is a part of our inherent nature. It is God's design.

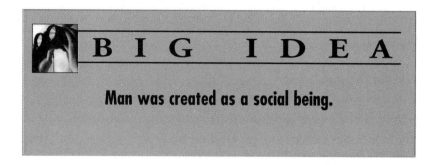

BIG IDEA

Man was created as a social being.

GOD MEETS OUR SOCIAL NEEDS

When Adam saw Eve, he recognized God's provision for his social needs. How is God providing for your social needs?

_____

_____

 ## PRAY ABOUT IT!

Write a prayer of thanksgiving to God for the special people He has brought within your social circle.

_____

_____

REVIEW KEY VERSE:

Colossians 3:15 *And let the peace of the Messiah, to which you were also called in one body, control your hearts. Be thankful.*

DAY 1 SUMMARY

How do we know that people are made to be "social beings"?

_____

_____

WEEK 7, DAY 2

WHAT'S WRONG WITH SOCIETY?

SOCIETY'S VITAL SIGNS

A medical doctor checks certain "vital signs" to determine a patient's health. This might include checking the pulse, blood pressure, and breathing. If these are within a certain range, the patient is considered healthy. But if one or more are outside normal limits, the patient has cause for concern.

Like an individual, a society has certain "vital signs" that indicate the condition of that culture. What might be some of those signs? Write as many as you can (the first is suggested for you):

Crime rate _____   _____

_____   _____

_____   _____

Below is a list of cultural vital signs. Circle one of the numbers on the scale after each area to indicate how you feel about the cultural health of our nation:

Healthy ◄————► *Sick*

Crime rate	1	2	3	4	5
Divorce rate	1	2	3	4	5
Stable families	1	2	3	4	5
Physical abuse	1	2	3	4	5
Drug/alcohol abuse	1	2	3	4	5
Sexual conduct	1	2	3	4	5
Education	1	2	3	4	5
Politics	1	2	3	4	5
Voter turnout	1	2	3	4	5
Volunteer organizations	1	2	3	4	5

So, how did you rate our society? Is it healthy or hurting? What was the average score? _____ (total of rankings ÷10)

DIAGNOSING THE PROBLEM

So what's the problem? Why is our society unhealthy? Let's go back to the medical analogy. When a patient has a fever, the doctor does not treat the fever. Do you know why?

_____

_____

The fever is not the problem. The fever is just a symptom of the real problem, which might be an infection in the body. The doctor treats the infection, not the fever. When it is eliminated, the fever goes away. Similarly, the disturbing social trends around us are only symptoms of an underlying problem. That brings us back to the question: What's the problem with society? Take a guess:

_____

_____

> *"If man's behavior were somehow conditioned by genetic code or social externals," says William Stanmeyer, "then no just judge could blame him for the evil he commits. But the scripture teaches unequivocally that God blamed Adam and Eve for succumbing to the temptation to disobedience and punished them accordingly."* (TLAC, 94)

There are basically three options as to the source of our social problems. Put a check by the source that is based on a biblical worldview:

- ❑ Genetic makeup

- ❑ External social pressure

- ❑ Individual sinful choices

> *The Christian view grants individuals much more control over society, but it also burdens them with much more responsibility. People, in the Christian perspective, must face the consequences of their decisions. This point is made painfully clear in the opening chapters of Genesis, when Adam and Eve bring a curse on the whole human race and are exiled from the garden of Eden, all because they choose to disobey God.* (TLAC, 93-4)

Re-read the above quote, and think about the implications of just two people's disobedience to God.

Disobeying God's moral principles not only brings negative consequences on the individual who breaks the moral code, but it also has a ripple effect throughout society. Like when a rock is thrown into a pond, the ripples eventually spread to the entire surface of the water.

Let's say that a local grocery store is robbed. Trace the ripple effect throughout the community when one person acts outside of God's moral law. What might be the consequences for each of the following people?

The thief: _____

The police officer: _____

The grocer: _____

The average shopper: _____

Local tax payers: _____

> ## 2 Corinthians 5:17
>
> *Therefore if anyone is in Christ, there is a new creation; old things have passed away, and look, new things have come.*

A SPIRITUAL CURE

Don't treat the symptom; treat the problem.

Most social problems originate from individual problems. Therefore, when we talk about the negative social trends we see today, we must address the fact that the solution is a moral and spiritual one for the individuals who make up society. A biblical worldview points to the cure for the problem of sin.

Read **2 Corinthians 5:17**. Write the verse in your own words:

_____

_____

The possibility for change is real. And when enough individuals change for the better, you will have a healthier society.

 ## PRAY ABOUT IT!

Write a prayer expressing your desire to be a part of the solution in building a healthy society.

_____

_____

DAY 2 SUMMARY

What is the root cause of social problems?

_____

WEEK 7, DAY 3

HOW TO CHANGE SOCIETY

A "BARN-RAISING" EXPERIENCE

If you were going to build a two-story barn to store your hay and to shelter your three cows and four horses (assuming, of course, that you actually owned three cows and four horses) . . . how long would you guess it would take to build an 8,000-square-foot barn all by yourself?

- ☐ Two weeks

- ☐ Two months

- ☐ Two years

- ☐ Too much for one person to do!

If you guessed "Too much . . .", you're right on the money. One person would have a tough time constructing a building that large.

Back in the "old" days, how did folks on the farm build a barn? They called on all of their neighbors and had themselves a good ol' fashioned "barn raising." What one person could not do by himself, the community of people could accomplish as a group.

As we've seen the last couple of days, social problems are actually a result of individual problems. Because the larger society is affected, it takes a community "barn raising" to bring about social change.

Yet in a "barn raising," everyone has a part. So now we have come full circle, to the individual as the solution. If individuals are the problem in society, then individuals must solve the problem.

CHRISTIANITY TO THE RESCUE

Recall the parable in the Bible of the Good Samaritan. Jesus told that story to show how we should be involved in meeting the needs of a hurting neighbor. Christians throughout the ages have taken Christ's teaching to heart and sought ways to help their neighbors—and their society. Let's take a brief survey from the beginning of the Christian church to see how this has taken place.

HOPE FOR CIVILIZATION

When the church was born, Roman civilization had brought peace and harmony to a large portion of the world. But within 400 years Roman culture fell to the sword of northern barbarians. During the next few centuries, chaos ruled Europe as warring bands of illiterate Germanic tribes opposed and deposed one another. Cities and cultural centers disappeared. Literacy, law, and order crumbled.

But one force prevented barbarism from completely taking over. What was that?

_____

It was the church! The medieval church modeled a counter-culture that kept the spark of civilization alive. Monks preserved not only the Scriptures but classical literature as well. They cleared land, built towns and harvested crops.

During the seventh century in France, the clergy were the best-educated and least immoral group in Europe. The French monks ran schools and sheltered orphans, widows, paupers and slaves. They constructed aqueducts, opened hospitals and were respected by a population staggering under the greed and dishonesty of their political leaders. The same was true in Ireland, England, and other countries of western Europe.[1]

Because Christians got involved in society, the barbarous Dark Ages gave way to the light of Christian culture, and civilization was renewed.

HOPE FOR HOLLAND

Don't curse the darkness . . . light a candle!

What is true in the general sweep of history is equally true in the lives of individual Christians who have sought to make a difference. Abraham Kuyper, a Dutch theologian and pastor in the early 1900's, provides an excellent example.

Kuyper worked diligently to influence public life in the Netherlands by founding a Christian university, publishing a newspaper, and even being elected prime minister. The social and educational reforms Kuyper initiated continue to benefit Holland today.[2]

Connect each area of society that Kuyper influenced with its corresponding worldview category:

A university	Philosophy
News reporting	Politics
Prime minister	Sociology
Social reforms	History

Why do you think Kuyper worked so diligently to influence these various social areas?

_____

_____

What was it about Kuyper's worldview that led him to social action?

_____

_____

To Kuyper, there were not two realms of reality—the secular and the sacred. If God created the world and people and societies, then everything in the world of people and societies relates to Him. Therefore, Kuyper became involved in helping society in specific ways.

CHANGED PEOPLE CHANGE THE WORLD

There is a connection between our biblical view of life and our view of society. Christianity is not just a "vertical" relationship with God; it also involves a "horizontal" relationship with other people.

In what ways can you influence your social world? Make a short list, and then ask God to direct your steps to be involved in a Christian "barn raising"!

(1) _____

(2) _____

(3) _____

DAY 3 SUMMARY

In what ways does Christianity influence society?

_____

REVIEW KEY VERSE:

Colossians 3:15 *And let the peace of the Messiah, to which you were also called in one body, control your _____. Be thankful.*

DIGGING DEEPER: *For more examples of how Christians throughout history have worked to change society for the better, see D. James Kennedy's* What If Jesus Had Never Been Born? *and* What If the Bible Had Never Been Written?, *or* Under the Influence: How Christianity Transformed Civilization, *by Alvin J. Schmidt (Zondervan Publishing House, Grand Rapids, 2001). Or, read Matt Kaufman's review of "Christianity on Trial" at:*

www.boundless.org/2001/regulars/kaufman/a0000528.html

WEEK 7, DAY 4

ALL IN THE FAMILY

Deuteronomy 6:1-2, 6-9

*6:1 Now this is the com-
mandment—the statutes
and ordinances—that the
LORD your God has com-
manded me to teach you
to observe in the land
that you are entering to
possess, ²so that you, your
son, and your grandson
may fear the LORD your
God and keep, all the
days of your life, all His
statutes and command-
ments that I am com-
manding you, so that
your life may be long.*

*6:6 These things that I
am commanding you
today are to continually
be in your minds.*

*⁷Repeat them to your
children, speak of them
when you are at home
and when you go on a
journey, when you lie
down and when you get
up. ⁸Bind them on your
hands as a sign, and let
them be a symbol on your
foreheads. ⁹Write them on
the doorposts of your
house and on your gates.*

WHY DID GOD MAKE FAMILIES?

The Bible makes it clear that families are a part of God's plan for mankind. But why did He do it that way? Can you come up with three practical reasons?

(1) _____

(2) _____

(3) _____

*For the Christian, marriage and the family are
ordained by God (Genesis 2:23-25) and together
will always be the fundamental institution of society.
The Christian believes that the family and its role
are strictly defined in the Bible.* (TLAC, 98)

The family has a unique ability to pass on traditions, history and discipline, and to provide a context for understanding the world.

Look at **Deuteronomy 6:6-9**, and list the different ways that parents are to instruct their children:

(1) _____   (5) _____

(2) _____   (6) _____

(3) _____   (7) _____

(4) _____   (8) _____

Now, an even more important question is: Why are parents to train their children by all of these methods? See **Deuteronomy 6:1-2**.

_____

_____

BIG IDEA

The first school of human instruction is the family!

Exodus 20:12

Honor your father and your mother so that your days may be prolonged in the land that the Lord your God is giving you.

It has been said, "repetition aids learning." If eight times a day you were hearing how God loves you and relates to everything you do, it would begin to sink in after a while!

WHAT'S A KID TO DO?

If parents are to do the teaching, then it just makes sense that children are to do the learning and obeying. Notice the fifth commandment (of the original ten!), in **Exodus 20:12**. What does God promise to children who honor their parents?

_____

Is this promise true? Check it out for yourself. Would a child lead a healthier and happier life if he obeyed the following instructions? If so, check the box:

Parent's instruction   Healthier/happier life?

Don't play in traffic . . . . ❑

Eat your spinach . . . . ❑

Share your toys with your sister . . . . ❑

Drive safely . . . . ❑

Don't take illegal drugs . . . . ❑

Save sexual intimacy for marriage . . . . ❑

Children may not like it at the time, but eating their spinach develops a healthier body. And a healthier child is a happier child. You can see that it really does make a difference if children obey their parent's instructions.

FAMILIES ARE IMPORTANT

Do families have an influence on society? Consider Jonathan Edwards—pastor, scholar, and leader of the First Great Awakening (a time of spiritual renewal in America in the 1700's). Jonathan and his wife Sarah left a remarkable legacy to American society. They raised 11 children, and by 1900, the family had 1,400 descendants, including:

> 13 college presidents
> 65 professors
> 100 lawyers
> 30 judges
> 66 physicians
> 3 governors
> 3 senators
> and
> A vice president of the United States![4]

This is what can happen when parents give moral and spiritual instruction, and children do the obeying—a healthy family tradition is passed down from generation to generation, and society benefits.

> *It is to society's advantage to build and encourage the God-ordained social institution of marriage and the family.* (TLAC, 98)

Studies agree with the biblical view of the family: marriage and families are important!

> After surveying more than 130 empirical studies, Professor Robert H. Coombs of the UCLA School of Medicine concluded: "Married people live longer and generally are more emotionally and physically healthy than the unmarried."[5]

WOW! Married people actually live longer!

PERSONAL REFLECTION

A saying goes: "If you want to marry a princess, you must first be a prince!" (Of course, the same holds true for you aspiring princesses out there.) What can you be doing now to develop into a prince or princess?

_____

_____

_____

DAY 4 SUMMARY

Give at least two reasons why families are so important.

_____

_____

_____

DIGGING DEEPER: *In recent years, our society has engaged in an ongoing debate over what constitutes a family. Research this topic to better understand the range of definitions for the family that are being promoted, how a worldview determines which side of this "culture war" one is on, and why it is important for a biblical worldview to prevail. You might start your investigation by reviewing articles found on www.leaderu.com and do a keyword search on "gay marriage" or "family."*

WEEK 7, DAY 5

CRIME, HEALTH, AND HAPPINESS

One historian researched church attendance in England over the years. During the times that more people attended Sunday school, what do you think happened?

☐ fewer people attended soccer games

☐ the crime rate went down

☐ the farmers grew more crops

☐ more people married

When Sunday school attendance was highest, the crime rate was lowest. And conversely, when church attendance was low, crime rose!

Going to church does make a difference! Not only does history bear this out, but recent surveys tell the same story:

> *Dr. Dale Matthews of Georgetown University reviewed 212 studies and found that three-fourths showed a positive effect of religious commitment on a person's health. The research shows that people who attend church are both physically healthier and less depressed.*[6]

You realize, of course, that just going and sitting in a pew is not what we are talking about. The key to success is believing and living biblical principles, not just warming a seat on Sunday mornings.

If you were to write a prescription for a happy, productive and healthy life based on the above statistics, what would it be?

_____

_____

_____

THE SOUL OF SOCIETY

The church also can cause a society to face God by providing an example of true community. If the Christian church could show the rest of society that it is possible to live according to the command "Love your neighbor as yourself," then individuals and society might be more willing to turn to God and acknowledge Him as the initiator of all relations. (TLAC, 99-100)

Think about that paragraph. What will cause some people to turn to God?

_____

_____

_____

THIS LITTLE LIGHT OF MINE

What happens when Christians retreat from being involved in society? Darkness. If we retreat from any area of our culture, the light flickers and goes out. All that is left is the darkness of man's ideas.

But Jesus has called us to spread His light of righteousness. The reason that we go to church and learn more about a relationship with God is so we can be equipped to proclaim His love to others who are still in darkness. Read **1 Peter 2:9** below:

But you are a chosen race, a royal priesthood, a holy nation, a people for His possession, so that you may proclaim the praises of the One who called you out of darkness into His marvelous light.

As a member of the church, how can you challenge the culture this week—at work, with your friends and neighbors, in your city? Really think about it, and list some ways:

(1) _____

(2) _____

(3) _____

PRAY ABOUT IT!

Review each summary statement from this week, and select three key areas to pray about:

Key concept	My prayer
(1) _____	_____
	_____
(2) _____	_____
	_____
(3) _____	_____
	_____

DAY 5 SUMMARY

What does the church offer society?

_____

_____

WEEK 7 SUMMARY: SOCIOLOGY

Biblical sociology focuses on three levels of society: the family, the church, and the state. All three, working together under God's direction, are needed for a healthy, safe, and sane society. Each level has its own purpose.

▼ The family is responsible for raising children and modeling godly living.

▼ The church is called to meet the larger needs of society in the areas of evangelism, education and social action.

▼ The state is designed to maintain order and administer justice.

REVIEW KEY VERSE:

Colossians 3:15 *And let the peace of the Messiah, to which you were also called in _____ _____, control your hearts. Be thankful.*

ENDNOTES
1. Charles Colson, *Against the Night* (Servant Books: Ann Arbor, Mich., 1989), p. 133-4.
2. Charles Colson, *A Dance with Deception* (Word: Dallas, Tex., 1993), p. 21.
3. *Against the Night*, p. 130.

4. *Breakpoint* with Chuck Colson, January 1997, p. 18.

5. *The Family in America*, Focus on the Family, June 1991, p. 2-3.

6. *"Several Studies Link Good Health With Religious Belief, Prayer"*, AP Wire Service, *Statesville Record & Landmark*, Tuesday, February 13, 1996, p. 8-A.

SCRIPTURE SUPPLEMENT

Genesis, Chapter 1:

[1]In the beginning God created the heavens and the earth.

[2]Now the earth was formless and empty, darkness was over the surface of the watery depths, and the Spirit of God was hovering over the surface of the waters. [3]Then God said, "Let there be light," and there was light. [4]God saw that the light was good, and God separated the light from the darkness. [5]God called the light "day" and He called the darkness "night." Evening came, and then morning: a first day.

[6]Then God said, "Let there be an expanse between the waters, separating water from water." [7]So God made the expanse and separated the water under the expanse from the water above the expanse. And it was so. [8]God called the expanse "sky." Evening came, and then morning: a second day.

[9]Then God said, "Let the water under the sky be gathered into one place, and let the dry land appear." And it was so. [10]God called the dry land "earth" and the gathering of the water He called "seas." And God saw that it was good. [11]And God said, "Let the earth produce vegetation: seed-bearing plants, and fruit trees on the earth bearing fruit, with seed in it, according to their kind." And it was so. [12]The land brought forth vegetation: seed-bearing plants according to their kind and trees bearing fruit with seed in it, according to their kind. And God saw that it was good. [13]Evening came, and then morning: a third day.

[14]Then God said, "Let there be lights in the expanse of the sky to separate the day from the night. They will serve as signs for the festivals and for days and years. [15]They will be lights in the expanse of the sky to provide light on the earth." And it was so. [16]God made the two great lights—the greater light to have dominion over the day and the lesser light to have dominion over the night—as well as the stars. [17]God placed them in the expanse of the sky to provide light on the earth, [18]to dominate the day and the night, and to separate light from darkness. And God saw that it was good. [19]Evening came, and then morning: a fourth day.

[20]Then God said, "Let the water swarm with living creatures, and let birds fly above the earth across the expanse of the sky." [21]So God created the large sea-creatures and all living creatures that move and swarm in the water, according to their kinds. He also created every winged bird according to its kind. And God saw that it was good. [22]So God blessed them saying, "Be fruitful, multiply, and fill the waters of the seas,

and let the birds multiply on the earth." ²³Evening came, and then morning: a fifth day.

²⁴*Then God said, "Let the earth produce living creatures according to their kinds: livestock, creatures that crawl, and the wildlife of the earth according to their kinds." And it was so. ²⁵So God made the wildlife of the earth according to their kinds, and the livestock according to their kinds, and creatures that crawl on the ground according to their kinds. And God saw that it was good.*

²⁶*Then God said, "Let us make man in our image and according to our likeness. They will rule the fish of the sea, the birds of the sky, and the animals and all the earth, and over the creatures that crawl on the earth."*

> ²⁷*So God created man in His own image;*
> *He created him in the image of God;*
> *He created them male and female.*

²⁸*God blessed them, and God said to them, "Be fruitful and multiply, fill the earth and subdue it. Rule the fish of the sea, the birds of the sky, and every creature that crawls on the earth."*

²⁹*God also said, "Look, I have given you every seed-bearing plant on the surface of the entire earth, and every tree whose fruit contains seed. This will be food for you ³⁰and for all the wildlife of the earth, for every bird of the sky, and for every creature that crawls on the earth that has the breath of life in it. Every green plant is for food." And it was so.*

³¹*And God saw all He had made, and it was very good. Evening came, and then morning: a sixth day.*

Genesis, Chapter 2:

¹*So the heavens and the earth and everything in them was completed. ²By the seventh day, God completed His work that He had done, and He rested on the seventh day from all the work He had done.*

³*God blessed the seventh day and declared it holy, for on it He rested from His work of creation.*

⁴*These are the records of the heavens and the earth when they were created, on the day that the LORD God made earth and heaven. ⁵No shrub of the field was in the land yet, and no plant of the field had sprouted yet, because the LORD God had not made it rain on the land and there was no man to work the ground. ⁶But a spring would come up from the land and would water all the surface of the ground. ⁷Then the LORD God shaped the man from the dust of the ground and breathed the breath of life into his nostrils, and the man became a living being.*

⁸*The LORD God planted a garden in Eden, in the east, and there He placed the man He had shaped.*

[9]And the LORD God caused to grow out of the ground every tree pleasing in appearance and good for food, including the tree of life in the midst of the garden, as well as the tree of the knowledge of good and evil. [10]And a river went out from Eden to water the garden. From there it divided and became the source of four rivers. [11]The name of the first was Pishon, which encircles the entire land of the Havilah, where there is gold.

[12]Gold from that land is pure; bdellium and onyx are also there. [13]The name of the second river is Gihon, which encircles the entire land of Cush. [14]The name of the third river is the Tigris, which flows to the east of Assyria. And the fourth river is the Euphrates.

[15]The LORD God took the man and placed him in the garden of Eden to work it and watch over it. [16]And the LORD God commanded the man saying, "You are free to eat from any tree of the garden, [17]but from the tree of the knowledge of good and evil you must not eat, for on the day you eat from it, you will certainly die."

[18]The LORD God said, "It is not good for the man to be alone. I will make a helping counterpart for him." [19]So the LORD God shaped from the ground each wild animal and each bird of the sky and brought each to the man to see what he would call it. And whatever the man called a living creature, that was its name. [20]The man gave names to all the livestock, to the birds of the sky, and to every wild animal; but for Adam no helping counterpart was found. [21]The LORD God caused a deep sleep to come over the man and he slept. God took one of his ribs and closed the flesh at that place. [22]Then the LORD God built the rib He had taken from the man into a woman and brought her to the man. [23]And the man said,

> This one at last is bone of my bone,
> and flesh of my flesh;
> this one will be called woman,
> for this one was taken from man.

[24]This is why a man leaves his father and his mother and bonds with his wife and they become one flesh. [25]The man and his wife were both naked and felt no shame.

NOTES

_____

_____

_____

_____

_____

_____

_____

_____

_____

_____

_____

_____

WEEK 8: LAW

WHY SO MANY LAWS?

Laws, laws everywhere and no place to hide! Everywhere you go there are laws. Driving down the highway requires obeying traffic laws. When you make money, there are laws that require you to pay a percentage in taxes. Your friends expect you to be truthful (that's a rule that everyone expects you to follow—if you don't think so, just try telling someone something that isn't true and let them find out!). In science, there are laws of chemistry, biology, and physics. Even in church there are rules for worshiping God (for example: we do not offer blood sacrifices on an altar; we do confess our sins to God). We are surrounded by laws!

When you think of "laws," do you have a positive or negative reaction? Many would say "negative!" But laws don't have to be bad. Why not?

It's simple, really. You'll remember back in our first week, we learned about the nature of God. God is Relational, yes. He is Righteous, certainly. But He also is RULER. God rules, and He designed the whole universe to work in sync with His character.

So everything is designed to operate according to the laws God established—laws of physics, laws of chemistry, laws of ethics, laws of civil government, laws of how to worship Him—it's all a package deal. We live in a world of laws. That's the way God designed it—and don't forget, God said that His design is good (Genesis 1:31)!

This week you will:

▼ Uncover the significance of the origin of laws
▼ Discern why we have laws and why laws are good to have
▼ Define what is meant by the term "natural law"
▼ Learn about biblical principles that rule our lives
▼ Explore the idea of "legislating morality"

WEEK 8, DAY 1

THE ORIGIN OF LAW

WHERE DO LAWS COME FROM?

Even in your earliest days, you discovered there are rules to live by. You heard mom or dad say, "Don't touch that hot stove!"—and it appeared that parents were the source of all the rules.

Then, as you grew older, you realized there is a larger world, and there are other sources for the rules that govern your life. List some of those other sources:

_____   _____

_____   _____

_____   _____

This leads to a very basic question: How do these people come up with all those rules? And per-haps another: What is the ultimate source for the rules that govern life? When you try to answer questions like this, you are dealing with the worldview category of law.

AND THE ANSWER IS: GOD!

> *The Christian believes that God has provided laws (and a means of discovering those laws) for mankind. "God is the only Legislator," says Carl F.H. Henry. "Earthly rulers and legislative bodies are alike accountable to Him from whom stems all obligation— religious, ethical and civil." (TLAC, 105)*

Henry mentions three areas in which God rules. Describe each one in your own words:

(1) Religious: _____

(2) Ethical: _____

(3) Civil: _____

When you consider these three realms, you are looking at all of life! There is no aspect of human interaction that is outside of God's domain.

ETHICAL LAWS

During our study of ethics, you discovered that the biblical view includes certain principles that govern our moral lives. These moral laws are just as binding and unchanging as the laws in the physical world. They are a part of the real world, the "totality of reality."

It doesn't matter whether you like it or not. Moral laws don't depend on "feelings." What do they depend on, and what should be your response?

_____

_____

CIVIL LAWS

Another area of law involves civil government. Consider **Genesis 9:6**, and respond to the following questions:

(1) If someone commits murder, who is responsible for seeking justice?

    ❏ God

    ❏ Society

    ❏ The physical world

(2) What is the reason given for repaying the murderer in this way?

_____

The basis for punishing a murderer is the fact that mankind is created in the image of God. As long as people are created in God's image, those that murder should be punished.

How long have people been created in God's image? _____

In the future, will people still be created in God's image? _____

If someone lives in the deep jungles of South America is he still created in God's image? _____

> ### Genesis 9:6
>
> *Whoever sheds man's blood, by man his blood will be shed, for in the image of God He made man.*

When they are based on eternal moral principles, civil laws have an unchanging foundation. They are just as real and constant as the law of gravity.

> *Society must decide whether an absolute legal standard exists. It does not matter whether society would prefer fixed or flexible laws. What matters is whether an absolute code is real. If such a code does exist, we must discover and obey it, for it points to a Law-giver worthy of our obedience and worship. The Christian, of course, believes such laws and such a Law-giver exist.* (TLAC, 107)

We see from this that the Bible explains why laws must exist. They exist because man is in rebellion against God and His law, so earthly laws and the means of punishment are required to curb or neutralize that rebellion.

LIVING SPIRITUALLY IN LIGHT OF GOD'S LAW

Meditate on **Hebrews 12:1-10** (see the Scripture Supplement on page 147) as it relates to being accountable to God for obeying His laws on every level: religious, moral, and civil. What insights do you see that encourage you to maintain a holy lifestyle?

_____

_____

_____

DAY 1 SUMMARY

What is the basis of "law"?

_____

_____

WEEK 8 KEY VERSE:

Colossians 1:17 *He is before all things, and by Him all things hold together.*

NOTE: The key verse for this week at first may not seem to relate to law. But the fact that Jesus Christ "holds together" everything is itself the basis for law. That's because not only do physical laws "hold together" the material universe, but moral and civil laws "hold together" society. They keep society from crumbling into chaos by making individuals accountable for their actions. You'll learn more about this aspect of law as you continue this week's study.

WEEK 8, DAY 2

LOOKING FOR LAW IN ALL THE WRONG PLACES

WHAT IF MAN MAKES THE RULES?

From our study of theology, we understand that God rules. And because He rules, we have laws to live by. But to get a clearer picture of the significance of God's laws, let's take a look at law from another angle. We can do that by asking the question: What if there is no God?

If we start with the assumption that God does not exist, that would mean that all moral and civil laws come from our own thoughts. What would be the result of this "human-centered" system of laws? Read the next quote carefully:

> Systems that deny God as Law-giver ultimately fail and will always adversely affect every individual mired in them. They fail because they recognize neither the dignity of man created in the image of God nor the fallen nature of man. If God does exist and does create law, then any society that ignores His laws will be out of step with reality. Further, a society or state that ignores God will promote arbitrary laws, consequently causing its subjects to lose respect for the legal system. John Whitehead believes that when fundamental principles of law are undermined, "public confidence in law and public willingness to abide by law are also sapped.". . . Without a law that is both unchanging and worthy of obedience, where can the individual discover a moral code (apart from mankind)? People quickly realize that if God does not exist, all things are permissible. (TLAC, 105-6)

The above paragraph states that "man-centered" systems of law will . . . (check the right answer)

❑ ultimately triumph

❑ be a positive benefit to mankind

❑ be more in line with reality

❑ ultimately fail

❑ have a more stable basis than a God-centered system

"Man-centered" systems of law will always fail because of five specific reasons. Summarize in your own words the five reasons given in the quotation on page 133:

(1) _____

(2) _____

(3) _____

(4) _____

(5) _____

THE LAW AND YOUR WORLDVIEW

These negative consequences start when we deny that God is the source of all law. Let's take another look at each of these areas to see how they relate to the ten worldview categories. Write in the blank the category that best corresponds to each phrase in the list below. This time we will state the phrases positively:

"Acknowledge God as Law-giver"   _____

"the dignity of man . . . the fallen nature of man"   _____

"in step with reality"   _____

"respect for the legal system"   _____

"public willingness to abide by law"   _____

"discover a moral code"   _____

Check your answers: God as Law-giver (Theology); the dignity of man and fallen nature (Psychology); in step with reality (Philosophy); the legal system (Politics); public willingness to abide by law (Sociology/Law); moral code (Ethics).

Once again it becomes clear: a consistent worldview affects every area of life.

BUT ARE LAWS "GOOD"?

You're talking to a friend when the conversation turns to a certain law just passed by Congress, and he says:

I understand that we have all of these laws and everything, but I still don't have a very good feeling about "laws" in general. I mean, they are so restrictive. I want to be free! I want to be me! I want to express myself in whatever way I feel without all of these restrictions. Laws are much too confining!

What would you say to your friend?

_____

_____

Can you think of an example from real life to explain why laws are good for us?

_____

_____

RESPONDING TO THE GOD WHO IS THERE

There are negative consequences for disobeying God's laws as well as positive results for individuals and society who obey them. When it comes to laws, "God knows best"!

Based on our study so far, is there any doubt in your mind that biblical Christianity paints for us a picture of the entire scope of reality and life? Over and over again, we come back to the fact that the Bible relates to all of life. You can't get away from God! He is concerned in a loving way with every part of your life.

Read **Psalm 139** (see the Scripture Supplement on pages 147-8) to catch a glimpse of how the author describes the wonder of knowing that God is there. Write the thoughts and feelings that come from your knowing that God is concerned with all of your life:

_____

_____

DAY 2 SUMMARY

Based on today's study, summarize why "man's own thoughts" is the wrong place to look for the source of law.

_____

_____

WEEK 8, DAY 3

DON'T TRY THIS AT HOME

If your friend says he has decided to step off the top of the Empire State Building just to see what happens, what would you tell him?

- ❏ You hope he has a nice flight.
- ❏ He is not living according to the real world.
- ❏ He is neglecting a basic principle of the universe: the law of gravity!
- ❏ He needs a "reality check"!

The last three statements would all be appropriate because if your friend tries his stunt, he will suffer the severe consequences of trying to live contrary to one of God's physical laws.

For example, the "law of gravity" explains a principle, built into the universe, that objects attract one another. Because gravity is a constant, the "law of gravity" is an accurate description of reality.

While the scientific method points us to the reality of physical laws, the question remains as to how we can know what is true when it comes to making laws that rule society.

DISCOVERING NATURAL LAW

To understand the basis for civil law, we must go back to the ancient Greek and Roman philosophers. For example, one of the most famous lawyers of ancient times was Cicero, who lived during the century before the birth of Jesus Christ. Cicero wrote, "True law is right reason in agreement with Nature. It is of universal application, unchanging and everlasting."[1]

Cicero understood something about the world. What was it that he knew about the law of nature?

_____

_____

Thomas Aquinas, the thirteenth-century Christian philosopher, wrote at length concerning this same idea, known as "natural law." The idea of natural law also was fundamental to our founders' understanding of political theory. It is mentioned in one of the primary founding documents of the United States of America, the Declaration of Independence, which refers to "…the laws of nature and nature's God."

BIG IDEA

A law is a principle that always holds true.

NATURAL LAW DEFINED

God reveals His law to people, in general, through natural law. Every person has a conscience, an inherent sense of right and wrong. (TLAC, 108)

Natural law, then, is defined as God's _____, revealed to man concerning what is _____ and _____.

In **Romans 2:14-15**, Paul writes that the Gentiles do not have the written law, such as the Ten Commandments. Yet, even they understand that certain things are right and certain things are wrong. How do they know?

- ❏ They read about it in the Bible.
- ❏ Their parents teach them.
- ❏ They find out by "trial and error."
- ❏ They have a conscience.

Now look at **Romans 1:18-22**. How does Paul describe "general revelation" in verse 20?

_____

Even though God made His presence known to man through nature (natural law), what was mankind's response?

_____

According to verses 21 and 22, by refusing to glorify and acknowledge God as the supreme ruler over life, man has suffered in what ways? _____

Romans 2:14-15

So, when Gentiles, who do not have the law, instinctively do what the law demands, they are a law to themselves even though they do not have the law. [15] *They show that the work of the law is written on their hearts. Their consciences testify in support of this, and their competing thoughts either accuse or excuse them . . . .*

Romans 1:18-22

For God's wrath is revealed from heaven against all godlessness and unrighteousness of people who by their unrighteousness suppress the truth, [19] *since what can be known about God is evident among them, because God has shown it to them.* [20] *From the creation of the world His invisible attributes, that is, his eternal power and divine nature, have been clearly seen, being understood through what He has made. As a result, people are without excuse.* [21] *For though they knew God, they did not glorify Him as God or show gratitude. Instead, their thinking became nonsense, and their senseless minds were darkened.* [22] *Claiming to be wise, they became fools . . . .*

Romans 1:24-32

Therefore God delivered them over in the cravings of their hearts to sexual impurity, so that their bodies were degraded among themselves. ²⁵ They exchanged the truth of God for a lie, and worshiped and served something created instead of the Creator, who is blessed forever. Amen.

²⁶ This is why God delivered them over to degrading passions. For even their females exchanged natural sexual intercourse for what is unnatural. ²⁷ The males in the same way also left natural sexual intercourse with females and were inflamed in their lust for one another. Males committed shameless acts with males and received in their own persons the appropriate penalty for their perversion.

²⁸ And because they did not think it worthwhile to have God in their knowledge, God delivered them over to a worthless mind to do what is morally wrong. ²⁹ They are filled with all unrighteousness, evil, greed, and wickedness. They are full of envy, murder, disputes, deceit, and malice. They are gossips, ³⁰ slanderers, God-haters, arrogant, proud, boastful, inventors of evil, disobedient to parents, ³¹ undiscerning, untrustworthy, unloving, and unmerciful. ³² Although they know full well God's just sentence—that those who practice such things deserve to die—they not only do them, but even applaud others who practice them.

IT'S FOOLISH TO REJECT GOD'S NATURAL LAW

> *. . . natural law explains why all people are considered accountable to God for their actions: because all are aware of the existence of a transcendent law and still consciously disobey it.* (TLAC, 108)

Read **Romans 1:24-32** for a list of some of the foolish behaviors people choose as a result of ignoring God's revealed laws. In what specific ways do you see these types of behaviors in your local schools, your community or the nation?

_____

_____

COMING OUT OF THE DARKNESS INTO GOD'S LIGHT

As a Christian, God has a better plan for you. Instead of living in spiritual and moral darkness, God has called you to a new life of freedom. According to **1 Peter 2:9** (see p. 139), what are the four phrases that God uses to describe you:

(1) _____

(2) _____

(3) _____

(4) _____

Why has He called you into "His marvelous light?"

_____

_____

How can you "declare His praises" this week?

_____

_____

DAY 3 SUMMARY

"Law" simply refers to a principle that is always _____.
Where does natural law come from?

_____

_____

WEEK 8 KEY VERSE:

Colossians 1:17 *He is* _____ *all things, and by Him all things*
_____ _____.

WEEK 8, DAY 4

GOD'S LAWS ARE GOOD FOR YOU

BE CAREFUL HOW YOU DRIVE!

Before anyone can drive a car, he or she must demonstrate knowledge of the rules of the road by studying the driver's manual and passing a test. Driving down the "road of life" requires the same attention to rules that govern life.

The Bible can be viewed as God's "Driver's Manual" for life. In its pages, He has given us the details for how we should live—the "rules of the road" for a safe and fulfilling life.

> God has made His law known to people through the Bible. Natural law provides a general concept of right and wrong, but the Bible fleshes out this skeletal framework so that people may know what God considers lawful. (TLAC, 109)

The Bible should not be viewed as just a boring old book of rules and regulations. The precepts in the Bible point the way to experience not only eternal life, but also a healthy and happy life here and now! So fasten your spiritual seatbelt, and get behind the Scripture wheel. You are about to embark on a joy ride using the life-enhancing Manual of Truth!

HERE'S TO YOUR HEALTH!

History holds some fascinating examples of the practical benefits of following the Manual of Truth.[2]

Example #1: During the sixth and seventh centuries, leprosy spread widely in Europe. By the fourteenth century, the human death toll from leprosy had reached a terrifying peak.

What did the physicians of the day do to stop the ever-increasing ravages of this disease? They thought that eating hot food, pepper, garlic and the meat of diseased hogs caused it. As you might imagine, their remedies were of no use.

About the same time, the Black Death began to ravage the land and took the lives of one out of four persons—an estimated sixty million. It is considered the greatest disaster of human history.

What brought an end to the major plagues of the Dark Ages? People turned to an idea they read in the Bible. Note **Leviticus 13:46**:

> He will be unclean as long as he has the infection. Since he is unclean, he must live alone; his dwelling must be outside the camp.

Summarize the answer they found there:

_____

_____

Example #2: Up until the late 1700's, it was the practice in most cities and towns to dump human waste into the streets. (Yuck!) Diseases like cholera, dysentery, and typhoid fever killed millions of people. Deliverance from these deadly epidemics came only when people began to apply two sentences from the Scriptures.[3] Summarize the basic principle of hygiene mentioned in **Deuteronomy 23:12-13**:

> *And there is to be a designated place outside the camp; you are to go outside there, [13]taking a spade in addition to your weaponry, and when you relieve yourself outside, you are to dig a hole with it, then turn and cover up your excrement.*

Example #3: In the 1840's, Vienna was famous as a medical center. Yet in the maternity wards of a well-known teaching hospital, one out of every six women died from infection. A similar mortality rate was observed in every other hospital. It was customary for the doctors to begin each day by visiting the morgue to perform autopsies. Then, without washing their hands, they would go into the maternity wards to examine the women there.

A doctor named Ignaz Semmelweis noticed the problem and started washing his hands in a basin of water before examining each patient. He saw dramatic results almost immediately, with very few women dying from infection.

 WORTH NOTING: Modern medical science is catching up to what the Bible has said all along!

Yet, many centuries before Semmelweis, God gave to Moses very detailed instructions on how to handle the dead. The biblical procedure was even more specific than Semmelweis used, and more effective. What were the additional factors needed to keep infection from spreading?[4]

Refer to **Numbers 19:16-19**, and answer the following:

After touching a corpse, a person must. . .

▼ _____ his clothes,

Genesis 2:24

This is why a man leaves his father and his mother and bonds with his wife and they become one flesh.

▼ bathe in _____,

▼ Wait for _____ days, and

. . . before being considered "clean."

These instructions are subsequently scientifically proven to deter the spread of infectious diseases. Yet Moses wrote down these principles over 3,000 years before modern medical "science"!

THE DARK AGES . . . PAST AND PRESENT!

The reason that the Dark Ages are called dark is that the light of the Bible was not widely known. For the most part, folks did not have access to the Scriptures. If people had been following these instructions all along, millions of lives would have been spared a lot of misery!

But guess what? Even though most people have access to the Bible today, we are still experiencing certain health-related problems, even here in the United States. The next example explains why.

Example #4: AIDS is a current health problem that is spreading rapidly around the globe. HIV, the virus that leads to AIDS, is contracted primarily through sexual contact.

Did you realize that we already have the cure for the spread of HIV? It is a simple practice that, if everyone followed it, would stop the majority of AIDS cases from ever developing. Do you know what would stop the spread of the AIDS virus?

_____

_____

The answer, again, is found in the Bible. It was God's idea in **Genesis 2:24** that a man and a woman should be united for life. God's Driver's Manual for Life goes on to warn about the dangers of sexual activity outside of a marriage covenant.

For example, **1 Corinthians 6:18** says:

Flee from sexual immorality! "Every sin a person can commit is outside the body," but the person who is sexually immoral sins against his own body.

Do you realize that sexual sin is not only immoral according to God's law, but it is also acting contrary to a known physical law against one's own body? That's because over 30 different kinds of sexually transmitted diseases can cause any of the following physical problems: high fever, vomiting, severe abdominal pain, agonizing pains in the muscles of the arms and chest (lasting for hours), sterility, birth defects, brain damage, blindness, deafness, heart attacks, insanity, and death!

Another thing you need to keep in mind is that sex outside of marriage goes against God's moral law. To commit sexual immorality is to invite God's judgment on your life.

GOD'S VIEW OF SEX

Does this mean that God is down on sex? Not at all. God's Driver's Manual is clear that sexual expression in marriage is designed to be a great joy and blessing. In fact, God suggests that a newly married couple take a one-year honeymoon! Check it out in **Deuteronomy 24:5**. (And by the way, the translation "bring joy to the wife" does not mean telling her jokes!)

God thought up the whole idea of sexual intimacy, and He knows how it works best. That's why He gave instructions for the most fulfilling way to experience His best: one man united with one woman for life!

TAKING THE DRIVER'S TEST

Read through **Proverbs 3:1-8** (see the Scripture Supplement on page 148), and make a list of the benefits of driving your life according to God's "rules of the road":

_____

DAY 4 SUMMARY

To what aspects of our lives does God's Driver's Manual for Life apply?

_____

_____

> ### Deuteronomy 24:5
>
> *When a man has recently married, he is not to go out with the army and will not be liable for any duty. He will be free to stay at home for one year so that he can bring joy to the wife he has married.*

WEEK 8, DAY 5

THE LAW ACCORDING TO HARRY

Harry S. Truman, our 33rd president, had this to say about the origin of the laws upon which the United States of America was founded:

> *The fundamental basis of this nation's law was given to Moses on the Mount. The fundamental basis of our Bill of Rights comes from the teaching which we get from Exodus and St. Matthew, from Isaiah and St. Paul. I don't think we emphasize that enough these days. If we don't have the proper fundamental moral background, we will finally wind up with a totalitarian government which does not believe in rights for anybody except the state.[5]*

What connection does Truman make between the Bible, law, morality, and government?

_____

_____

According to Truman:

Can you have government without morality? _____

Can you have morality without law? _____

Can you have law without the Bible? _____

While a society could have laws without the Bible, these laws would be man-made, and there would be no reason for people to obey the laws except to keep from being punished if caught.

On the other hand, the Bible gives a basis for truly moral laws. Government's role, then, is to translate these moral laws into civil law. So, there is a direct link from the Bible to government, by way of natural law and biblical morality.

THE FOUNDATION FOR LAW

> *For the Christian, law is grounded on the firmest foundation and therefore does not flex or evolve. Whitehead insists that "Law has content in the eternal sense. It has a reference*

point. Like a ship that is anchored, law cannot stray far from its mooring." The Christian perspective creates a legal system that does not fluctuate according to the whims of people and, therefore, it creates a system that is more just. (TLAC, 107)

The above text comments on a certain quality of law. What is unique about the Christian legal perspective compared to other systems of law?

_____

_____

What would make this system of law more just than other systems?

_____

_____

PROTECTING HUMAN RIGHTS

In one sense, law and morality are inseparable. When one declares theft illegal, one is making a moral judgment—theft is condemned as immoral, because it violates divine law. . . . People must concentrate on formulating a legal system that legislates morality only to the extent that order is maintained and human rights are protected. (TLAC, 114-5)

Issues like abortion and homosexual marriage are more than just legal issues. They deal with more than a woman's right to reproductive choice or the right to privacy for two consenting adults. The long-standing civil laws upon which these issues rest have traditionally been based on natural law.

But since 1973, the courts in the United States have claimed that a woman has a "right" to her own body. Therefore, it is further claimed that she can abort a pregnancy if she desires. How would you evaluate this idea through the lens of a biblical worldview?

_____

_____

If, as the Bible claims, man is created in the image of God, then each human life becomes inestimably precious and meaningful. This, in turn, creates a firm foundation on which a system of human rights can be built. (TLAC, 112)

If human life is "inestimably precious," what does this imply about the issue of abortion?

_____

_____

 WORTH NOTING: If people are made in the image of God, that has serious implications for abortion.

Human rights are not founded on society's changing ideas, but on the fact that people are created in the _____ of God.

But in recent years, these civil laws have been changing. Why?_____

_____

_____

Our lawmakers are moving away from the biblical basis of natural law. Civil laws, ripped from their foundation, have been set adrift in a sea of relativity and human whims.

ACTION POINT

What can you do to stop this trend away from natural law? Brainstorm several possibilities for yourself:

_____

_____

Share these ideas with a few close friends and family members.

DAY 5 SUMMARY

What is the connection between biblical and civil law?

_____

_____

DIGGING DEEPER: *Abortion is still a source of major legal and political battles in our country. What are the key issues when it comes to abortion? For a concise treatment of abortion on demand, see Dr. Frank Beckwith's four-part article, "Abortion, Politically Correct Death?," found at www.summit.org, go to Resources, then to Subjects, then to Abortion.*

WEEK 8 KEY VERSE

Colossians 1:17 *He is before all things, and by Him _____ _____ hold together.*

WEEK 8 SUMMARY: LAW

Another piece of the worldview puzzle falls into place: Law. "Natural law" is the idea that God has created the universe to run on certain principles that are true for everyone and everything. These laws govern the physical universe as well as the moral, spiritual and civil areas of life. Laws are not to be avoided but are rules to live by, designed by God for our individual good and for the good of society.

ENDNOTES

1. Quoted in *The Roots of American Order,* Russell Kirk (Regnery Gateway, Washington, D.C., 1991), p. 108.

2. S.I. McMillen, *None of these Diseases* (Fleming H. Revell Co., Old Tappan, N.J., 1963), p. 11-2.

3. Ibid., p. 12-3.

4. Ibid., p. 14-6.

5. William J. Federer, *America's God and Country Encyclopedia of Quotations* (Fame Publishing, Inc, Coppell, Tex., 1994), p. 589-90.

SCRIPTURE SUPPLEMENT

Hebrews 12:1-10 *Therefore since we also have such a large cloud of witnesses surrounding us, let us lay aside every weight and the sin that so easily ensnares us, and run with endurance the race that lies before us, [2]keeping our eyes on Jesus, the source and perfecter of our faith, who for the joy that lay before Him endured a cross and despised the shame, and has sat down at the right hand of God's throne.*

[3]For consider Him who endured such hostility from sinners against Himself, so that you won't grow weary and lose heart. [4]In struggling against sin, you have not yet resisted to the point of shedding your blood. [5]And you have forgotten the exhortation that addresses you as sons:

My son, do not take the Lord's discipline lightly, or faint when you are reproved by Him;

[6]for the Lord disciplines whom He loves, and punishes every son whom He receives.

[7]Endure it as discipline: God is dealing with you as sons. For what son is there whom a father does not discipline? [8]But if you are without discipline—which all receive—then you are illegitimate children and not sons. [9]Furthermore, we had natural fathers discipline us, and we respected them. Shouldn't we submit even more to the Father of spirits and live? [10]For they disciplined us for a short time based on what seemed good to them, but He does it for our benefit, so that we can share His holiness.

Psalm 139 *LORD, You have searched me and known me.*
[2]You know when I sit down and when I stand up; You understand my thoughts from far away.
[3]You observe my travels and my rest; You are aware of all my ways.
[4]Before a word is on my tongue, You know all about it, LORD.
[5]You have encircled me; You have placed Your hand on me.
[6]This extraordinary knowledge is beyond me. It is lofty; I am unable to reach it.
[7]Where can I go to escape Your Spirit? Where can I flee from Your presence?
[8]If I go up to heaven, You are there; if I make my bed in Sheol, You are there.

[9]*If I live at the eastern horizon or settle at the western limits,*

[10]*even there Your hand will lead me; Your right hand will hold on to me.*

[11]*If I say, "Surely the darkness will hide me, and the light around me will become night"—*

[12]*even the darkness is not too dark for You. The night shines like the day; darkness and light are alike to You.*

[13]*For it was You who created my inward parts; You knit me together in my mother's womb.*

[14]*I will praise You because I am unique in remarkable ways. Your works are wonderful, and I know this very well.*

[15]*My bones were not hidden from You when I was made in secret, when I was formed in the depths of the earth.*

[16]*Your eyes saw me when I was formless; all my days were written in Your book and planned before a single one of them began.*

[17]*God, how difficult Your thoughts are for me to comprehend; how vast their sum is!*

[18]*If I counted them, they would outnumber the grains of sand; when I wake up, I am still with You.*

[19]*God, if only You would kill the wicked (stay away from me, you bloodthirsty men)*

[20]*who invoke You deceitfully. Your enemies swear by You falsely.*

[21]*LORD, don't I hate those who hate You, and detest those who rebel against You?*

[22]*I hate them with extreme hatred; I consider them my enemies.*

[23]*Search me, God, and know my heart; test me and know my concerns.*

[24]*See if there is any offensive way in me; lead me in the everlasting way.*

Proverbs 3:1-8 *My son, don't forget my teaching, but let your heart keep my commands;*

[2]*for they will add to you many days, a full life, and well-being*

[3]*Never let loyalty and faithfulness leave you. Tie them around your neck; write them on the tablet of your heart.*

[4]*Then you will find favor and high regard in the sight of God and man.*

[5]*Trust in the LORD with all your heart, and do not rely on your own understanding;*

[6]*consider Him in all your ways, and He will clear your paths.*

[7]*Do not be wise in your own opinion; fear the LORD and turn away from evil.*

[8]*This will be healing for your body and strengthening for your bones.*

WEEK 9: POLITICS

EVERYBODY'S GOT RIGHTS . . . RIGHT?

Why do some women abort their pre-born children? Because they claim a legal "right" to their own bodies. Why do some people try to stop the construction of a new dam? Because they claim that a small fish in one of the creeks has a legal "right" to its own habitat. Why do some people take the school district to court if a teacher has a Bible on his desk in the classroom? Because they claim a legal "right" to separate "church and state."

You read about them everywhere: Women's rights, gay rights, abortion rights, civil rights, animal rights. . . it seems that everybody and everything has rights! We hear so much about "rights," but what happens when someone else's "rights" step on your "rights"? And who's to say which rights are the right rights? And–funny thing–you hear all this talk about "rights" but not very much about "responsibilities."

Only a biblical Christian worldview can sort through the maze of rights and balance them with a correct understanding of our responsibilities. The answer to the rights issue is found in a biblical view of "politics."

Politics, the art of governing a city, state, or nation, answers the question: What should be the structure and role of government? This week you will add the politics piece of the puzzle to a complete biblical Christian worldview.

We will confront some ideas that are controversial in our society today. That's because many people are moving away from a biblical understanding of these issues. But we will seek God's perspective and principles to guide us toward the best political system.

This week will put you on the right track to understanding what's wrong (and right) with rights. During the daily sessions, look for:

▼ How God relates to government

▼ How our human nature dictates what type of government is best

▼ The purpose of government

▼ Why religion and politics do mix, and

▼ When you should obey the government and when you should not!

WEEK 9, DAY 1

GOVERNMENT AND GOD

---

1 Corinthians 14:40

But everything must be done decently and in order.

ONLY TWO (MAYBE THREE?) THINGS ARE CERTAIN

The saying goes, "There are only two things for certain—death and taxes."

Actually, we could add a third to that list: death, taxes, and *government!*

But why government? Because government has been around as long as death and taxes!

We usually think of death and taxes as something to be avoided. Does that make government as bad as the other two? Our understanding of biblical sociology revealed that God established the state as one of the three main institutions of society. And the reason He did that is a theological one.

But how does government reflect the nature of God? The next few pages explore this connection between God and government.

IT ALL STARTS WITH GOD

In the first place, God is a God of order. He always does things in an orderly manner. Examples of this are found throughout the Bible.

For instance, when God created the heavens and the earth, He did it in an orderly fashion. In fact, the universe is called the cosmos. *Cosmos* is a Greek word that means order. It is the opposite of chaos, which means disorder.

Furthermore, God gave commandments for how we should order our lives morally. And in the New Testament, order was a concern of Paul.

Read **1 Corinthians 14:40**. What does Paul say must be done in order?_____

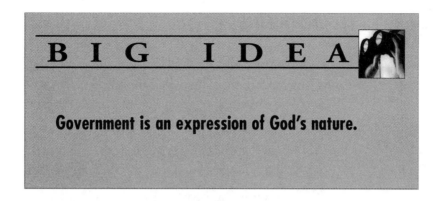

BIG IDEA

Government is an expression of God's nature.

CAN WE GET A LITTLE ORDER AROUND HERE?

How does the Godly characteristic of order relate to government? What do you think?

To help you with your answer, reflect on this: What if there were no government, no laws, no police, no courts, no common laws such as highway speed limits, no civil authority whatsoever? What would life be like? Check your answer:

- ❏ Cosmos
- ❏ Chaos
- ❏ Confining
- ❏ Cooperative

Government should adhere to the principle "everything must be done decently and in order" (1 Corinthians 14:40; Exodus 18:19f) since this is a reflection of God's character. Further, it should be participatory, so that Christian citizens can better influence the state to conform to God's will as a social institution (Proverbs 11:11). (TLAC, 123)

Government is necessary to keep individuals from infringing on the rights of others. Therefore, government is . . . (check the right choice)

- ❏ A "necessary evil" in the world.
- ❏ An after-thought of God.
- ❏ A positive good for mankind.
- ❏ Neither positive nor negative; it just is!

Government, as a reflection of God's nature, is designed to be a positive good by keeping order in society so people can live peaceful and tranquil lives. But there is a second relationship between God and government.

Exodus 23:6 *Do not deny justice to your needy in their lawsuits.*	

SEEKING JUSTICE

The idea of justice also comes from the nature of God. We discussed it regarding theology when we asked: What is God like? Which of the three major characteristics of God relates to God's justice?

❏ God is Ruler

❏ God is Relational

❏ God is Righteous

Being just, or righteous, is a central aspect of God's character. God's justice means that He always judges fairly. And He requires that we reflect His nature by being just with our fellow man, too.

> *Most everyone believes that furthering justice is an important task of the state, but the Christian sees justice as the principal reason for the state's existence. Such a view of justice is grounded in an absolute Guarantor of unalienable rights. Because of this, promoting justice becomes more important than any other aspect of government.* (TLAC, 126)

PAUSE TO REFLECT

Reflect on **Exodus 23:6**, and list some reasons why justice is an important aspect of government.

_____

_____

DAY 1 SUMMARY:

What two roles of government reflect specific facets of God's nature?

(1)_____

(2) _____

WEEK 9 KEY VERSE

Colossians 3:25 *For the wrongdoer will be paid back for whatever he has done wrong, and there is no favoritism.*

WEEK 9, DAY 2

GOVERNMENT AND MAN

A TALE OF TWO ISLANDS

Imagine that you are responsible for governing the inhabitants of two islands. On one island, Island A, you have people who are good-natured, hard-working, family-oriented, and honest. On the other, Island B, the people are violent, lazy and greedy.

As you look into the future, which of these two islands would you predict would have the greatest prosperity and individual freedom?

- ❑ Island A
- ❑ Island B

Which of the two islands will require the most laws, policemen and prisons?

- ❑ Island A
- ❑ Island B

Based on the above scenario, summarize your thoughts on why both God and government are needed:

_____

_____

WHY WE NEED GOVERNMENT (PART 2)

Yesterday we made the connection between God and the need for government. Government is a reflection of God's character, specifically His o_____ and j_____.

But government not only reflects the character of God, it also conforms to the nature of man.

GOVERNMENT AND HUMAN NATURE

Perhaps the Christian concept America's founders best understood was the Christian view of human nature. The United States was born in an environment in which men held a Christian view of mankind's fallen nature, but they did not forget that people are created in the image of God. These two beliefs have profound implications for a Christian view of politics, which is reflected in America's founding fathers' attempts to tailor a government suited to mankind's place in God's creative order. (TLAC, 124)

America's founders had a unique opportunity to design a completely new political system. As they began their task, they took seriously the biblical worldview of psychology. What two aspects of human nature did they consider important?

(1) Mankind is created in God's _____ .

(2) Mankind has fallen into _____ .

 WORTH NOTING: "If men were angels, no government would be necessary."
—James Madison, 4th President of the United States

These ideas concerning man's basic nature provided the foundational principles for our national government, a government that—while certainly not perfect—has proven to give more freedom and opportunity to its citizens than any other governmental system in history.

HUMAN RIGHTS . . . AND *RESPONSIBILITIES!*

The fact that these unalienable rights have an unchanging Source is crucial for Christian politics. If rights were not tied inextricably to the character of God, then human rights would be arbitrarily assigned according to the whims of each passing generation. Rights are "unalienable" only because they are based on God's unchanging character. God established government to secure these rights. This protection of human rights is God's basic purpose for government. (TLAC, 125)

Think about it: Since human rights come from God, they are "unalienable," which means that only _____ can change them or take them away.

And if God is the source of our rights, He is also the source of our responsibilities. These are the moral standards that must guide our day-to-day lives and decisions.

Our founding fathers clearly understood this connection between God, man and government. Read the following quote from James Madison, signer of the Declaration of Independence and the main author of the U. S. Constitution:

We have staked the whole future of the American civilization, not upon the power of government, far from it. We have staked the future. . .upon the capacity of each and all of us to govern ourselves, to control ourselves, to sustain ourselves according to the Ten Commandments of God.[1]

DOES IT STILL APPLY TODAY?

James Madison acknowledged the need for the people of our nation to control themselves according to the Ten Commandments, yet some people today say that the Ten Commandments should not even be posted on the walls in a public school. What do you think about the legal status of publicly posting the Ten Commandments?

_____

_____

Some people say that a woman has a right to her own body. Therefore, she has the right to abort an unwanted pregnancy. How would you evaluate this legal right from the standpoint of a biblical worldview?

_____

_____

If accepting Jesus Christ as one's personal Savior and Lord leads a person to accept his responsibility to obey God's laws, and obeying God's laws leads to good government, what can you do to promote good government?

_____

_____

DAY 2 SUMMARY

What two aspects of human nature support the need for government?

(1)_____

(2)_____

WEEK 9, DAY 3

THE PURPOSE OF GOVERNMENT

GODLY GOVERNMENT

A Scripture passage that outlines the purpose of government is found in **Romans 13:1-7**. Read it over (see page 157), and fill in the following blanks:

▼ In verses 3 and 4, what are the two ways the state is to function?

    (1) To _____ those who do right.

    (2) To _____ those who do wrong.

▼ These two basic functions of the state, to commend the good and punish the evil, come from the _____ which God has established (verse 1).

▼ Because state authorities are established by God, we should _____ to them (verse 5).

▼ Submitting to government means to give what is due to those that rule, including _____, _____, _____, and _____ (verses 6-7).

From a biblical perspective, the purpose of the state is to punish those who break the law and praise those who obey the law. Evaluate your local, state or national government by listing how it is fulfilling these two functions (check a newspaper or news magazine for examples).

An example of government punishing an evildoer is:

_____

An example of government praising someone who does good is:

_____

A GOOD QUESTION

But who protects society from its rulers?

> *Thus, government protects mankind from its own sinful nature. But who protects the society from the sinful inclinations of those who make up the government? This was the problem with which America's early leaders grappled in attempting to create a just political system.* (TLAC, 124)

Politics brings with it a very sticky problem: If people are our rulers and people are basically sinful, then who protects society from the "sinful inclinations" of those who rule?

How did America's early leaders address the problem?

_____

The founding fathers built into the U.S. Constitution a unique system that keeps people in power only for short periods of time and allows for the orderly transition of power to new leaders. In that way, power is not concentrated in the hands of just a few people. And since government leaders are elected by the people at large, those leaders have an obligation to rule fairly or they may be dismissed.

THE FOURTH BRANCH OF GOVERNMENT

> *The aspects of American government that most closely conform to the Christian ideal are, not surprisingly, the most valuable part of America's political heritage. These include America's division of governmental power into three branches—legislative, executive, and judicial—and the concordant system of checks and balances.* (TLAC, 123-4)

You are aware of the three branches of government, but you might say there are actually four "branches" that make our government function properly. The fourth branch of our government is "We, the people. . . !" Yes, the citizens of the United States act as a fourth branch of government.

Our role is to elect Godly leaders and hold them accountable for their actions either by continuing to re-elect them or by voting them out of office. We have the ultimate obligation to "check and balance" the power of our elected officials.

THE SCOPE OF GOVERNMENT

> *Government, according to this [the biblical Christian] view, has limited responsibility. The state should concentrate on enforcing justice and avoid meddling in the business of other institutions. It must never assume the responsibilities of other institutions, including church and family.* (TLAC, 126)

Romans 13:1-7

Everyone must submit to the governing authorities, for there is no authority except from God, and those that exist are instituted by God. [2]So then, the one who resists the authority is opposing God's command, and those who oppose it will bring judgment on themselves. [3]For rulers are not a terror to good conduct, but to bad. Do you want to be unafraid of the authority? Do good and you will have its approval. [4]For government is God's servant to you for good. But if you do wrong, be afraid, because it does not carry the sword for no reason. For government is God's servant, an avenger that brings wrath on the one who does wrong. [5]Therefore, you must submit, not only because of wrath, but also because of your conscience. [6]And for this reason you pay taxes, since the authorities are God's public servants, continually attending to these tasks. [7]Pay your tolls to those you owe tolls, respect to those you owe respect, and honor to those you owe honor.

Limited government was the vision of the early leaders in America. The state should stick to its purpose and not interfere in the affairs of _____ or _____. This allows the maximum amount of freedom for all people.

Evaluate the current situation in the United States. Does the state interfere with areas that belong to the church or family? If so, in what ways?

_____

_____

GOVERNMENT AND YOU

Specifically, what can you do to help government (local, state, or national) function in the way that God designed it to?

_____

_____

DAY 3 SUMMARY

What are the basic functions of government supposed to be?

_____

_____

How is the system of government in the United States designed to protect people from the sinful tendencies of the people in power?

_____

_____

WEEK 9 KEY VERSE:

Colossians 3:25 *For the wrongdoer will be _____ _____ for whatever he has done wrong, and there is no favoritism.*

WEEK 9, DAY 4

RELIGION AND POLITICS

THE MAKING OF THE CONSTITUTION

The men who founded our nation were in a unique position. They had the opportunity to start a new government from scratch. Before them were a blank piece of paper and the history of man's efforts to govern himself.

If you had been one of the delegates to the Constitutional Convention back in 1787, what principles would you have written into the Constitution?

_____

_____

RELIGION AND THE FOUNDING FATHERS

The founders of the United States designed the federal government to operate according to certain principles. Did they intend for religion to play a part in this great "experiment in freedom"? What do you think?

❑ Yes, the founders saw the importance of government being based on specifically biblical Christian religious principles.

❑ No, the founders meant to separate the state from religion.

❑ The founders thought that religion should be a personal, private belief but not play any role in running the country.

To answer the above question, it's necessary to get into the minds of the founders. The following is a brief summary of some of the thoughts and opinions of these men. Can religion be separated from government? Their words give the answer.

George Washington (1732-1799) was president of the Constitutional Convention and the first president of the newly formed United States of America. He said during his farewell address after his second term in office:

> _Of all the dispositions and habits which lead to political prosperity, religion and morality are indispensable supports. . . ._[2]

According to Washington, what are the two necessary supports of any political system?

1) _____

2) _____

"Popular government" refers to our political system where people vote for their officials. What is necessary for this type of government?

_____

Why do the people who make up a nation need to be moral?

_____

Patrick Henry (1736-1799), while best known for his "give me liberty or give me death" speech, also helped write the Constitution of Virginia, served as a member of the Continental Congress, and was a five-time governor of the State of Virginia. Look at his words:

> *It cannot be emphasized too strongly or too often that this great nation was founded, not by religionists, but by Christians; not on religions, but on the Gospel of Jesus Christ. For this very reason peoples of other faiths have been afforded asylum, prosperity, and free-dom of worship here.*[3]

The U.S. was not founded on just any religion, but on the _____ religion. Yet this has not led to narrow-minded religious bigotry toward other religions. What has been the result, according to Henry?

_____

_____

Thomas Jefferson (1743-1826) was the primary author of the Declaration of Independence and our third president. He wrote in 1781:

> *God who gave us life gave us liberty. . . . Indeed I tremble for my country when I reflect that God is just; that his justice cannot sleep forever.*[4]

Jefferson mentions two things about God. First, God is the source of _____. And second, God is _____.

Liberty and justice are two key goals of government. Is Jefferson saying that a nation cannot have liberty or justice apart from God? From a biblical worldview, why is that the case?

_____

John Quincy Adams (1767-1848), at the age of fourteen, was appointed by Congress as Ambassador to Russia. He also served as a U.S. senator, U.S. minister to France and Britain, secretary of state for President James Monroe and as the sixth president of the United States. On July 4, 1821, he said in a speech:

> *The highest glory of the American Revolution was this; it connected in one indissoluble bond the principles of civil government and the principles of Christianity.*[5]

What does "indissoluble" mean? _____

According to John Quincy Adams, what two things are inseparable in the American system of government?

(1) _____

(2) _____

Literally hundreds more such examples could be given, but this brief sampling gives you the basic drift of the thinking of those men who designed the government of the United States.

DAY 4 SUMMARY

By now you should have a pretty good understanding of the relationship between religious principles and politics. Write a short summary based on the ideas of America's founders:

_____

_____

DIGGING DEEPER: *It is clear that the vast majority of the founding fathers of the United States held to a deeply ingrained biblical worldview. Yet some skeptics in recent years have claimed that the founders intended to write a "secular" constitution for our nation. Is this the case? You might begin research on this issue by reading the article, "A Godless Constitution?" found at www.wallbuilders.com. Go to Issues & Articles, and then Search for the title of the article.*

WEEK 9, DAY 5

THE QUESTION OF OBEDIENCE

Romans 13:5

Therefore, you must submit, not only because of wrath, but also because of your conscience.

Acts 4:19

But Peter and John answered them, "Whether it's right in the sight of God for us to listen to you rather than to God, you decide; . . ."

WHAT WOULD YOU DO?

You are living in Germany during the 1940's. The government has ordered all Jews to be taken away from the city and sent to death camps. Your best friend, who is a Jew, comes to your door one night and asks to come in. She tells you that her parents and siblings were picked up by the secret police that afternoon while she was away from the house. She doesn't know what to do, where to go, whom to trust.

What do you do? Read **Romans 13:5** and **Acts 4:19** before selecting one of the following options:

- ❒ Help her by hiding her in your basement.
- ❒ Tell her to go somewhere else.
- ❒ Call the secret police to report where she is.

Did you struggle with the two passages from the Bible? There seems to be a conflict: Do you obey the government according to Romans 13:5, or do you disobey the authorities as Acts 4:19 suggests? How do you know which command in the Bible to obey when the commands seem to contradict each other?

THE "GREATER COMMAND" PRINCIPLE

The solution to the dilemma may be found in **Matthew 22:37-39**. Jesus said that the _____ command is to love God, and the _____ is to love your neighbor. This suggests that some commands take priority over others.

Jesus established the principle of the greater command. In other words, when there is a conflict between two commands in Scripture, you should obey the "greater" one.

In the following examples, determine which is the greater command to obey.

B I G   I D E A

Obey the greater command.

He [Jesus] said to him, "'You shall love the Lord your God with all your heart, with all your soul, and with all your mind.' [38] *This is the greatest and most important commandment.* [39] *The second is like it : 'You shall love your neighbor as yourself.'"*

Example #1: Two nations are at war. A woman living in a town controlled by the corrupt government is hiding some spies from the other nation. Military officers come to her door and ask if she knows where the spies are hiding. What should she do?

❏ Colossians 3:9 says to not lie, so she should tell the truth by showing the authorities where the spies are hiding.

❏ Exodus 20:13 says to not murder, so she should lie to the authorities in order to save the lives of the spies.

(Joshua 2 and Hebrews 11:31 give an example of a similar real-life situation with Rahab.)

EXAMPLE #2: The government passes a law to control population growth. Nurses are ordered to kill certain newborn babies and allow others to live. What should the nurses do?

❏ Romans 13:5 says to submit to civil authorities, so they should kill the newborns. They won't be held accountable by God because they are just obeying orders.

❏ Exodus 20:13 says to not murder, so the nurses should not kill any of the babies, and if necessary, lie to the government to conceal their actions.

(Exodus 1:15-20 explains the historical event behind this dilemma involving the king of Egypt and the Hebrew midwives.)

You can see from these two biblical examples that the greater principle is to save a life, even if it means disobeying civil authorities.

This demonstrates how a consistent worldview helps you to understand how to handle life's situations. Here we combined ethics (how we determine the moral thing to do) with politics (how we relate to government) and arrived at the answer to our initial dilemma regarding hiding our friend from the Nazis.

> ### Proverbs 29:2
>
> *When the righteous flourish, the people rejoice, but when the wicked rule, people groan.*

YOU AND GOVERNMENT

> *. . . the Christian is called to obey the government, to honor justice, and to preserve order. However, this does not mean that Christians must obey government blindly. The political leader has a responsibility to God, and the Christian must hold him accountable.* (TLAC, 129-30)

Proverbs 29:2 is very instructive regarding your responsibility as the fourth branch of government. Summarize the verse in your own words:

_____

DAY 5 SUMMARY:

What principle guides our decision on how to respond to right and wrong demands of government?

_____

WEEK 9 KEY VERSE:

Colossians 3:25 *For the _____ will be paid back for whatever he has done wrong, and there is no favoritism.*

WEEK 9 SUMMARY: POLITICS

The starting point for every political system is its religious foundation, specifically, its theology and philosophy. The purpose of the state is to bring order to society and to administer justice, which assumes certain ethical standards. Psychology relates to politics because man's sinful tendencies require a balance of power in government. A biblical sociology determines that the state has a limited function and should not interfere with the family and the church. And lastly, natural law and the Bible are the basis for making the laws of the land. It all forms a consistent and total picture—a biblical worldview of politics!

ENDNOTES

1. William J. Federer, *America's God and Country Encyclopedia of Quotations* (Fame Publishing: Coppells, Tex., 1994), p. 411.

2. *Original Intent,* David Barton (Wallbuilder Press: Aledo, Tex., 1996), p. 116.

3. *America's God and Country Encyclopedia of Quotations*, p. 289.

4. Ibid., p. 323.

5. Ibid., p. 18.

WEEK 10: ECONOMICS

MAKING MONEY BY THE BIBLE!

Don't let the term economics fool you. It may sound stuffy, but it deals with an area that is near and dear to your heart. It has to do with how you get what you want and keep what you get! More specifically, it deals with how we exchange goods and services. Have you ever thought about how the economy in America works and how it is different from other nations of the world? We enjoy a standard of living that is one of the–if not the–highest in the world. And it's not just because we have more natural resources. Other countries have similar ones, but their people live in relative poverty. Why the difference?

It's because the founders of our nation used biblical principles to establish how people could make and use money. The founders' biblical Christian worldview informed their economic principles.

"Economics" comes from Greek–*ecos*, meaning "house," and *nomos*, meaning "law." It is the "law of the household." Our earlier study of law revealed that God designed the universe to work according to certain laws or principles. This is true for the world of nature (physical laws), ethics (moral laws), and even legal concerns (civil law). But there are also economic "laws" that determine the best way to "get what we want." Based on the nature of God (He is just) and the nature of man (made in God's image, yet sinful), a picture of these basic economic principles begins to emerge.

The main principle of biblical economics is "free exchange." That means people should be free to produce goods and services (legally, of course) and sell them as they choose. History has proven that "free and peaceful exchange" (also called a free market), more than any other system of economics, allows the greatest amount of material wealth and well-being for the greatest number of people.

This week you'll be introduced to:

▼ Practical lessons on work from the Seven Dwarfs

▼ The Bible's view on "big" government

▼ The need to own things

▼ Other practical tips on God's view of money and godly living

WEEK 10, DAY 1

WORK IS A WAY OF LIFE

LESSONS FROM THE SEVEN DWARFS

Remember "Snow White and the Seven Dwarfs"? What a cool story! Think about those little guys, the seven dwarfs. With a whistle and a song, they would "heigh-ho" to work in the mine each day.

What do you think we can learn about work from the seven dwarfs?

_____

_____

Those little storybook characters can teach us a couple of things. The first is this: Each day it's "off to work we go." Work is a daily routine for all of us in some form or another.

And second, since work is unavoidable, you might as well enjoy it! You may not feel like whistling while you work, but it sure does make the time go better.

 CONSIDER THIS!
Work is a natural and necessary part of life, so you might as well enjoy it!
And . . . these two ideas come right out of the Bible!

A BIBLICAL VIEW OF WORK

Way back at the beginning of human history, God placed Adam and Eve in a beautiful garden. Think about this: When was the idea of "work" first introduced to mankind?

_____

Some people associate work with God's punishment for Adam after he sinned, but the Bible actually paints a different picture. Look at **Genesis 3:17-19**, and answer the following questions:

What was the consequence of Adam's sin?

_____

God's curse on the ground meant that it would now produce what?

_____

What words are used to describe Adam's labor?

_____

_____

So is "work" God's curse on mankind?

_____

_____

No, "work" is not the curse. Check out **Genesis 2:15:**

> The LORD God took the man and placed him in the
> garden of Eden to work it and watch over it.

Notice: This is before Adam sinned! God placed Adam in the garden to "work it and take care of it." Work was a part of God's original plan–His "good" plan for Adam before his fall. God designed life in such a way that we are involved in His creation. A theologian once said, "God even milks the cow through you."

So work is not a curse. It is a part of God's blessing and design for mankind. We are designed to work. Only after the fall did this blessing become a hardship.

WORK HAS ITS REWARDS

> After casting Adam and Eve out of Eden, God decreed
> that mankind must face a life of toil (Genesis 3:17-19).
> But God, in His mercy, allowed that people who
> conscientiously adhere to this duty may be rewarded
> with private property. Proverbs 10:4 states, "Whoever
> works with a lazy hand becomes poor, but a diligent
> hand brings riches." God has designed a world in
> which the existence of private property encourages
> people to be responsible and fruitful. (TLAC, 137)

Look at **Proverbs 10:4** (stated in the above quote) and re-write it in your own words:

_____

_____

Genesis 3:17-19

> And to Adam He said, "Because you listened to your wife's voice and ate of the tree about which I commanded you, 'Do not eat of it': the ground is cursed because of you. Through painful labor you will eat from it all the days of your life.
> [18] It will produce thorns and thistles for you, and you will eat the plants of the field.
> [19] You will eat bread by the sweat of your brow until you return to the ground, since you were taken from it. For you are dust, and you will return to dust.

Exodus 20:9-11

Six days you may labor and do all your work, [10]but the seventh day is a Sabbath to the Lord your God. On it you must not do any work—you, your son or daughter, your male or female slave, your livestock, or your foreigner who is within your city gates. [11]For in six days the Lord made the heavens and the earth, the sea, and everything in them; then He rested on the seventh day. For that reason the Lord blessed the Sabbath day and made it holy.

Proverbs 12:14

From the fruit of his mouth, a man will be satisfied with good, and a man's hands will bring a profit to him.

Proverbs 21:25

A slacker's craving will kill him because his hands refuse to work.

Does this mean that everyone who works hard will become wealthy?

_____

_____

The Bible does not promise lots of material riches, but it does convey the idea that we should keep what we earn. This is important and will be explored more on Day 2.

BUT DO I HAVE TO LIKE IT?

Do you have to "like" work? Of course not! But since it's a way of life, you might as well enjoy it. Look over the following verses to get God's perspective on work. Write the thoughts that come to you from each passage.

Exodus 20:9-11 _____

_____

_____

Deuteronomy 16:13-15 _____

_____

_____

Deuteronomy 24:19 _____

_____

_____

Proverbs 12:14 _____

_____

_____

Proverbs 21:25 _____

_____

_____

PUTTING IT ALL TOGETHER

What can you conclude from the above Bible study regarding how to make a living? Write a summary:

_____

_____

DAY 1 SUMMARY

Work is a _____ and _____ part of life, so you might as well _____ it.

How do you know work itself is not a curse from God?

_____

_____

WEEK 10 KEY VERSES

Colossians 3:23-24 *Whatever you do, do it enthusiastically, as something done for the Lord and not for men, [24] knowing that you will receive the reward of an inheritance from the Lord–you serve the Lord Christ.*

Deuteronomy 16:13-15

You are to celebrate the Festival of Booths for seven days after you have gathered in the produce from your threshing floor and your winepress. [14] You are to rejoice during your festival—you, your son, your daughter, your male and female slaves, the Levite, the foreign resident, the fatherless, and the widow within your city gates. [15] For seven days you are to celebrate a festival to the LORD your God at the place the LORD will choose. For the LORD your God will bless you in all your harvest and in everything you put your hand to, and you will have nothing but joy.

Deuteronomy 24:19

When you reap the harvest in your field and forget a sheaf in the field, do not go back to get it. It should be left for the foreign resident, the fatherless, and the widow, so that the LORD your God may bless you in all the work you do.

WEEK 10, DAY 2

PRIVATE OWNERSHIP

You could always count on Molly to make things interesting, and this particular morning was no exception. The Tuesday Morning Bible Club had been studying the book of Acts, and Molly had something to say. So in her customary way, she blurted out, "I've got a question! Jesus' disciples living in Jerusalem shared everything they had, right? So why don't Christians do that today? If we're really serious about following the Lord, why don't we form a commune and share everything in common?"

Everyone in the Bible study sat there in silence, not knowing exactly how to respond. What do you think about Molly's question? Should Christians refuse to own anything privately and instead share everything like one big family?

How would you respond to Molly?

_____

_____

CHRISTIANITY AND SOCIALISM

> *Christians are divided on the issue of economics. While many Christians believe the Bible encourages an economic system of private property and individual responsibilities and initiatives (citing Isaiah 65:21-2; Jeremiah 32:43-4; Acts 5:1-4; Ephesians 4:28), many others are adamant in their support for a socialist economy (citing Acts 2:44-45).* (TLAC, 135)

As it turns out, Molly is not alone. There are some Christians who call for a "socialist" system where everyone shares equally in the economic "pie." They advocate for government, through centralized planners, to regulate the way people work and do business in order to distribute wealth more evenly to all citizens.

Do you see how easy it is to link economic and political ideas? You really can't separate the two. It's natural to talk about them together. So our question is now between two options:

(1) Should the government be in control of the way people make and use their resources, property, or money (a system called socialism or communism)?

(2) Should the government protect economic freedom to allow the peaceful exchange of goods and services (called a free market economy)?

THE BIBLE AND PRIVATE PROPERTY

Look at **Acts 2:44-46** where it describes how the first Christians lived together. Is this a pattern that we should follow today?

_____

_____

Why or why not? _____

_____

As it turns out, the passage in Acts 2 is a special situation with Jews coming to Jerusalem from every known nation (Acts 2:5– *There were Jews living in Jerusalem, devout men from every nation under heaven*). Notice how the Christians took care of each other (circle the word that best fits in the blank):

(1) The early believers _____ sold some of their property (Acts 2:46–some still had houses) and pooled their resources. (voluntarily / under compulsion)

(2) There was _____ government agency forcing anyone to contribute. (no/ a big)

(3) This was an illustration of Christian _____ rather than state welfare policy. (charity/ coercion)

What do you conclude about what this passage teaches concerning private property?

_____

_____

_____

_____

_____

Acts 2:44-46

Now all the believers were together and had everything in common. ⁴⁵So they sold their possessions and property and distributed the proceeds to all, as anyone had a need. ⁴⁶And every day they devoted themselves to meeting together in the temple complex, and broke bread from house to house. They ate their food with gladness and simplicity of heart, . . .

> ## 1 Kings 4:25
>
> *All the days of Solomon, Judah and Israel from Dan to Beer-sheba lived in safety, everyone under his vine and under his fig tree.*
>
> ## Jeremiah 32:44
>
> *People will buy fields with silver, draw up deeds, seal them, and have them witnessed in the land of Benjamin, in the areas surrounding Jerusalem, and in Judah's towns—the towns of the hill country, the towns of the Judean foothills, and the towns of the Negev. For I will restore their fortunes declares the LORD.*

PRIVATE OWNERSHIP: A BIBLICAL OVERVIEW

But God has an even broader perspective of private property. Check out the following:

1 Kings 4:25 says that each man lived under his own _____ and ____ _____. (Private property refers to anything that a person owns, not just land!)

Jeremiah 32:44 indicates a future time when the nation of Israel will be free to _____ and _____ property.

In **Acts 5:1-4**, was Peter angry because Ananias owned property or because he lied about what he had?

_____

What is your conclusion about God's view of private property? Check your answer:

❑ God's design is for people to share all things in common.

❑ It's not clear from the Bible what we should do related to private ownership.

❑ The biblical view indicates that people have the right to own things privately and exchange them peacefully and freely.

PRACTICAL CHRISTIAN PRINCIPLES

A nation that follows Christian principles has practical benefits. Look in the paper for examples of people living in socialist-controlled countries and compare their situation with that of people living in free market economies. What factors contribute to whether people prosper or live in poverty?

_____

_____

The United States was founded on the biblical principles of a free market and private ownership. This has led to building a nation whose people have one of the highest standards of living ever attained.

Do people work harder when they are: (A) Allowed to keep the fruit of their labor, or (B) Required to place their earnings in a common storehouse?

_____

_____

_____

NOTE: If you are involved in a group study, bring your articles to the next meeting and discuss the implications with your friends.

DAY 2 SUMMARY

From our study of politics, you'll recall that one of the functions of government is to provide justice. What role does that mean the government should play in making sure people have what they need economically?

_____

_____

_____

Acts 5:1-4

But a man named Ananias, with Sapphira his wife, sold a piece of property. ²However, he kept back part of the proceeds with his wife's knowledge, and brought a portion of it and laid it at the apostles' feet. ³Then Peter said, "Ananias, why has Satan filled your heart to lie to the Holy Spirit and keep back part of the proceeds from the field? ⁴Wasn't it yours while you possessed it? And after it was sold, wasn't it at your disposal? Why is it that you planned this thing in your heart? You have not lied to men but to God!"

WEEK 10, DAY 3

STEWARDSHIP

THE BIBLE AND STEWARDSHIP

Psalm 24:1

The earth and everything in it, the world and its inhabitants, belong to the LORD

Yesterday's study considered the biblical view of private property. There is another side to that coin, and that is stewardship. Read the following quotation for insight into this important concept.

> Beisner states, "Biblical stewardship views God as Owner of all things (Psalm 24:1) and man individually and collectively as His steward. Every person is accountable to God for the use of whatever he has (Genesis 1:26-30; 2:15). Every person's responsibility as a steward is to maximize the Owner's return on His investment by using it to serve others (Matthew 25:14-30)." (TLAC, 137)

Read **Psalm 24:1**. Everything belongs to _____. Think of the world as God's "garden" and people as the managers of it. We are accountable to Him for how we use His natural resources and for what we produce with our work.

We all work in His garden, either directly or indirectly. What types of work would be direct involvement in God's garden?

_____

Direct involvement includes things like farming and raising animals. But it is also the use of natural resources, including various kinds of technology, manufacturing and production (like construction, clothes, cars, and computers). These activities take the natural resources found in God's world and reshape them for our care, comfort and convenience. In other words, direct involvement includes all legal and moral activities that better the human condition.

Indirect involvement in God's garden includes the support services associated with the above activities. Examples of these are insurance, sales, business management, and education.

MONEY IS A SPIRITUAL THERMOMETER

So you are involved in God's garden one way or another. Somehow, you earn money by your work. Money is simply a convenient means of exchange for acquiring material things that other people work to produce. Therefore, how we spend money reflects how we manage the resources God has provided for us.

Jesus told a story about using money wisely, but He had a spiritual purpose behind the story. Read the entire parable in **Matthew 25:14-30** (see the Scripture Supplement on pages 183-4), and reflect on the following questions:

Who does the master represent? _____

If God is the master, who are the servants? _____

If we are the servants, what do the "talents" represent?

_____

If the talents relate to the things that God has given us, such as personal abilities that we can use for His kingdom, what is the main point that Jesus is making in this story?

_____

_____

Jesus shows that money is our spiritual thermometer. A thermometer provides an objective way to determine a person's body temperature. Similarly, how you make and spend money and how you use your God-given abilities are objective ways to determine your spiritual condition.

How are you doing with the wise use of the abilities that God has given to you?

_____

_____

_____

What can you do this week to be a more faithful steward in God's

> ## Proverbs 22:1-2,7,9
>
> *A good name is to be chosen over great wealth; favor is better than silver and gold. [2] The rich and the poor have this in common: the LORD made them both. [7] The rich rule over the poor, and the borrower is a slave to the lender. [9] A generous person will be blessed, for he shares his food with the poor.*

kingdom?

_____

_____

APPLYING GOD'S WISDOM TO YOUR LIFE

God's wisdom book has many practical ideas on how to handle your money. Look at the selected verses from **Proverbs 22** (see page 175), and write each idea in your own words:

vs. 1 _____

vs. 2 _____

vs. 7 _____

vs. 9 _____

DAY 3 SUMMARY

How does our use of money and personal resources reflect our spiritual condition?

_____

_____

WEEK 10 KEY VERSES

Colossians 3:23-24 *Whatever you do, do it enthusiastically, as something done for the _____ and not for men, [24] knowing that you will receive the reward of an inheritance from the Lord—you serve the _____ Christ.*

WEEK 10, DAY 4

SOCIAL JUSTICE

RICH MAN, POOR MAN

Molly (the one in the Tuesday morning Bible study) still isn't satisfied. She goes on, "You know, the Bible says that we should love and care for one another, especially the poor. Look at all of those millionaires and wealthy corporations that make all of that money. It's not fair. Wouldn't it be more compassionate to pass laws to tax the rich so the government can provide ways to help the poor?"

How do you respond this time to Molly's question?

_____

_____

In a way, Molly has a point. What could be more noble than helping the poor? Should Christians strive for "economic equality" among all people?

ECONOMIC EQUALITY: A NOBLE NOTION?

How does Paul's example and command in **2 Thessalonians 3:7-13** (see the Scripture Supplement on page 184) relate to the issue of whether we should seek economic equality?

_____

_____

If a person is able to work and doesn't, then he does not deserve to eat! That may sound harsh, but let's see how this plays out from a biblical worldview.

WORLDVIEW ANALYSIS

What have you learned so far that would help you evaluate Paul's principle of "earning what you eat"?

(Theology) God's righteous nature includes the quality of justice. He is always fair. Is it fair to take money from one person and give it to another? Why not?

_____

_____

Leviticus 19:9-10

When you reap the harvest of your land, do not reap to the very edges of your field or gather the gleanings of your harvest. ¹⁰Do not go over your vineyard a second time or pick up the grapes that have fallen. Leave them for the poor and the alien. I am the Lord your God.

1 Timothy 5:8

Now if anyone does not provide for his own relatives, and especially for his household, he has denied the faith and is worse than an unbeliever.

(Psychology) Considering that mankind is basically sinful, how would you expect people to act when they are given something for nothing (i.e., under a system of welfare)?

_____

_____

(Politics) Should the state take money from some people in order to give it to others (i.e., tax the wealthy to feed the poor)? What's the biblical purpose for government?

_____

_____

(Sociology) If government is not designed to redistribute wealth, then what social institutions have responsibility for looking after people in need?

_____

_____

(Economics) Now consider what the Bible has to say about God's design for work from the study on Day 1. Who is responsible to work for what they have?

_____

_____

How does this plan benefit the owner of the fields?

_____

_____

How is this biblical plan for helping those in need different from the state-run welfare programs used today?

_____

_____

God did not design welfare for people in need. Instead, you might call His the first "workfare" program. In God's economy, people are instructed to work for a living. His provision of gleaning allows a person in need to work for himself or herself and gather their own food. In **Ruth 2** (see the Scripture Supplement on pages 184-5), we see a real-life example of this principle in action. Read it for yourself.

This same theme is repeated in the New Testament. Note **1 Timothy 5:8** and write out the warning connected with the importance of looking after your own family:

_____

_____

CAUSES OF PROVERTY

What can you do to reduce poverty? Read **1 Timothy 6:17-19** to find out. (By the way, compared to the rest of the world, you are rich, so these verses do apply to you!)

Based on 1 Timothy 6:17-19, list some of the attitudes and actions that will put you in a position to help the poor:

(1) _____

(2) _____

(3) _____

> ### 1 Timothy 6:17-19
>
> *Instruct those who are rich in the present age not to be arrogant or to set their hope on the uncertainty of wealth, but on God, who richly provides us with all things to enjoy.* [18]*Instruct them to do good, to be rich in good works, to be generous, willing to share,* [19]*storing up for themselves a good foundation for the age to come, so that they may take hold of life that is real.*

DAY 4 SUMMARY

Why is the goal of enforcing "economic equality" for everyone not consistent with God's plan?

_____

DIGGING DEEPER: *Thomas Jefferson wrote, "Were we directed from Washington when to sow and when to reap, we should soon want bread" (Understanding the Times, p. 663). Evaluate this principle in light of the history of the early pilgrims and more recent socialist nations such as the former Soviet Union, China, or Cuba. If this is true with the production of food, does the same principle relate to other issues such as healthcare, retirement planning, or education? Give examples and statistics to back up your answer. To aid your thinking in this area, view the article, "Socialism, Capitalism, and the Bible," by Ron Nash at:* www.summit.org. *Go to Resources, then Subjects, then Economics*

WEEK 10, DAY 5

ECONOMICS AND FREEDOM

FREEDOM OR SECURITY?

The year is 2025, and there is a national poll being taken to determine the economic direction of our nation. You must decide between the following two options:

(1) Freedom: You will be free to live where you want, choose your own work and own your own things.

(2) Security: You will be assured food, shelter and a guaranteed job, arranged by the government.

What are the positive and negative points for you and for society of choosing freedom?

Positives: _____

Negatives: _____

What are the positive and negative points for you and for society of choosing security?

Positives: _____

Negatives: _____

If you had to choose one, which would it be? (circle your choice)

Freedom   Security

Clearly, there is a relationship between the type of economy a society chooses and the amount of freedom the individual must sacrifice. In a socialist society, the individual must relinquish to the government much of the control over his life. "The only way to arrive at equal fruits is to equalize behavior," says Beisner, "and that requires robbing men of liberty, making them slaves." (TLAC, 142)

According to Beisner, if you choose security over freedom, you lose your liberty and become a _____ to the state.

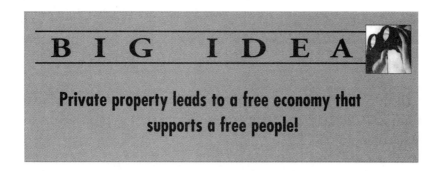

BIG IDEA

Private property leads to a free economy that supports a free people!

ECONOMIC FREEDOM LEADS TO POLITICAL FREEDOM

Economic freedom and the right to private property are crucial for political freedom.
(TLAC, 143)

Restate in your own words how these three areas interrelate: economic policy, personal freedoms, and politics.

_____

_____

As we discovered during our journey into politics, it's in the nature of governments to control people. That's why our founders sought to reign in the state's potential for abusing individual liberty by creating separate branches of government. But there are two other ways government is kept in check.

One is economic freedom. Economic freedom allows the development of private institutions, such as businesses, universities, and civic associations. These are important because they help disperse the ability of a too-powerful state to control people.

Second, private property is crucial to hold the state in check. How does private property serve to balance the power of government?

_____

Think about it: If you can buy a printing press or TV station or sell newspapers, you have the opportunity to tell other citizens about what government officials are doing. If elected officials become corrupt or try to take too much power, then a "free press" can report this, and the offending politicians can be voted out of office.

But what would happen if there were no private property and the government owned all the printing presses and radio/TV stations and controlled what news was distributed?

_____

_____

This is exactly what happened in Nazi Germany during World War II. The people of Germany and the rest of the world did not know that Hitler was sending Jews to death camps until toward the end of the war. That is because there was no free press; Hitler controlled the news media.

 CONSIDER THIS! The same is true when it comes to education. Government-controlled education gives the state the ability to use curriculum as propaganda to train children to think a certain way.

Again, recall that Hitler and Stalin used the schools to spread socialism and allegiance to their ideology. So, a biblical worldview that connects economic freedom, private property and political freedom is very important, to say the least.

PUTTING THE PIECES TOGETHER

According to **Ephesians 4:28,** *The thief must no longer steal. Instead, he must do honest work with his own hands, so that he has something to share with anyone in need.*

How does Ephesians 4:28 summarize the principles that you have learned about a biblical view of economics?

_____

_____

DAY 5 SUMMARY

How would giving up freedom in exchange for security ultimately result in the loss of security as well?

_____

_____

_____

WEEK 10 KEY VERSES

Colossians 3:23-24 *Whatever you do, do it _____, as something done for the Lord and not for men, [24] knowing that you will receive the _____ of an inheritance from the Lord—you serve the Lord Christ.*

WEEK 10 SUMMARY: ECONOMICS

When it comes to economics, God has the best ideas. First of all, God has designed us to work. Even though work may be difficult because of Adam's sin, we can still enjoy being involved in God's garden. Secondly, through work we gain possessions that we can use to freely and peacefully exchange for other things that we need or desire. The biblical worldview directs us to a free market system that allows the greatest personal freedom to make and spend money and to improve our own economic situation. And third, we should be willing to share our abundance and our experience with those who need to learn to help themselves. As the saying goes: Give someone a fish and he is fed for a day; teach someone to fish and he is fed for a lifetime.

SCRIPTURE SUPPLEMENT

Matthew 25:14-30 *"For it is just like a man going on a journey. He called his own slaves and turned over his possessions to them. [15]To one he gave five talents; to another, two; and to another, one to each according to his own ability. Then he went on a journey. Immediately [16]the man who had received five talents went, put them to work, and earned five more. [17]In the same way the man with two earned two more. [18]But the man who had received one talent went off, dug a hole in the ground, and hid his master's money.*

[19]*"After a long time the master of those slaves came and settled accounts with them [20]The man who had received five talents approached, presented five more talents, and said, 'Master, you gave me five talents. Look, I've earned five more talents.'*

[21]*"His master said to him, 'Well done, good and faithful slave! You were faithful over a few things; I will put you in charge of many things. Enter your master's joy!'*

[22]*"The the man with two talents also approached. He said, 'Master, you gave me two talents. Look, I've earned two more talents.'*

[23]*"His master said to him, 'Well done, good and faithful slave! You were faithful over a few things; I will put you in charge of many things. Enter your master's joy!'*

[24]*"Then the man who had received one talent also approached and said, 'Master, I know you. You're a difficult man, reaping where you haven't sown and gathering where you haven't scattered seed. [25]So I was afraid and went off and hid your talent in the ground. Look, you have what is yours.'*

[26]*"But his master replied to him, 'You evil, lazy slave! If you knew that I reap where I haven't sown and gather where I haven't scattered, [27]then you should have deposited my money with the bankers. And when I returned I would have received my money back with interest.*

[28]*"'So take the talent from him and give it to the one who has ten talents. [29]For to everyone who has, more will be given, and he will have more than enough. But from the one who does not have, even what he has will be taken away from him, [30]And throw this good-for-nothing slave into the outer darkness. In*

that place there will be weeping and gnashing of teeth.'"

2 Thessalonians 3:7-13 *For you yourselves know how you must imitate us: we were not irresponsible among you; [8]we did not eat anyone's bread free of charge; instead, we labored and toiled, working night and day, so that we would not be a burden to any of you. [9]It is not that we don't have the right to support, but we did it to make ourselves an example to you so that you would imitate us. [10]In fact, when we were with you, this is what we commanded you: "If anyone isn't willing to work, he should not eat." [11]For we hear that there are some among you who walk irresponsibly, not working at all, but interfering with the work of others. [12]Now we command and exhort such people, by the Lord Jesus Christ, that quietly working, they may eat their own bread. [13]But you, brothers, do not grow weary in doing good.*

Ruth 2:1-23 *Now Naomi had a relative on her husband's side, from Elimelech's family, a man of wealth and influence. His name was Boaz.*

[2]Ruth the Moabite said to Naomi, "I would like to go to the fields to gather leftover grain behind someone who shows me favor."

Naomi replied to her, "Go, my daughter."[3]So she departed. She came and gleaned in the field behind the harvesters. By chance she came to the portion of field that belonged to Boaz, who was from Elimelech's family.

[4]Just then, Boaz arrived from Bethlehem and said to the harvesters, "May the LORD be with you."

They replied, "May the LORD bless you."

[5]Then Boaz said to his servant who was in charge of the harvesters, "Who does this young woman belong to?"

[6]The servant in charge of the harvesters answered, "She is the young Moabite woman who returned with Naomi from the land of Moab. [7]She said, 'May I please glean and gather among the sheaves behind the harvesters.' She came and has been on her feet from early morning until now, except that she sat in the shelter for a little while.

[8]Boaz said to Ruth, "Listen, my daughter. Don't go to glean in another field, and don't leave this one, but stay here with my young women. [9]Keep your eyes on the field where they are harvesting, and follow them. I have ordered the young men not to touch you. When you're thirsty, go to the water jars and drink from what the servants have drawn."

[10]So she bowed with her face to the ground and said to him, "Why have I found favor with you that you have noticed me, when I am a foreigner?"

[11]Boaz answered her, "I've been told about all you've done for your mother-in-law after your husband's death—how you left your father and mother, and the land of your birth, and how you came to a people you didn't know before. [12]May the LORD reward your work, and may you be richly repaid by the LORD God of Israel, under whose wings you have come for refuge."

[13]Then she said, "May I find favor with you, my lord, for you have had compassion on me, and you have spoken kindly to your servant, although I am not the equal of your servants."

[14] At mealtime Boaz said to her, "Come here and eat some of the food and dip your bread in the vinegar." She sat beside the harvesters and he offered her roasted grain. She ate and was satisfied, and had some left over.

[15] When she got up to glean, Boaz ordered his young men, "She may glean even among the sheaves, and don't harass her. [16] Pull some stalks out of the bundles for her. Leave them for her to glean, and don't rebuke her. [17] So she gleaned in the field until the evening. Then she beat out what she had gleaned, and there were about 30 pounds of barley.

[18] She picked it up and went into the city, and her mother-in-law saw what she had gleaned. Ruth brought out what she had left over from her meal and gave it to her.

[19] Then her mother-in-law said to her, "Where did you glean today, and where did you work? May the one who noticed you be blessed."

She told her mother-in-law about the one she had worked with and said, "The name of the man I worked with today is Boaz."

[20] Naomi said to her daughter-in-law, "May he be blessed by the LORD, who has not forsaken His kindness to the living or to the dead." Naomi continued, "The man is a close relative; he is one who can redeem us."

[21] Then Ruth the Moabite said, "Besides, he told me, 'Stay close to my young men until they have finished all of my harvest.'"

[22] So Naomi said to her daughter-in-law Ruth, "It is good, my daughter, for you to go with his young women; then no one can harm you in another field."

N O T E S

WEEK 11: HISTORY

DRY BONES OR DYNAMIC IDEAS?

"Don't know much about history . . ."

That's a line from a song in the 'seventies.' It could be the theme song for many students today. The reason history seems so boring is that the focus is usually on names, places and dates. But these are only the dry bones of history. The real lifeblood of history is *ideas*.

Once you grasp the ideas of history, the relevance of history comes alive. Why? Because the ideas people have do not change very much over time. The details change, the technology changes, but the basic ideas remain the same.

The apostle Paul writes that the events of the Old Testament "happened to them as examples, and they were written as a warning to us. . . ." **(1 Corinthians 10:11)**. We can learn valuable lessons from the experiences of others.

But more than that, a biblical Christian worldview gives us a context for understanding history. The Bible points to a definite progression of events. Its story line begins in the "beginning," flows through time, and climaxes at the resurrection of Jesus. Even our calendars attest to the change from B.C. (Before Christ) to A.D. (Anno Domini, meaning "In the year of our Lord").

The Bible also points to the future, a time when God will draw to a close this earthly story and bring to account the lives and actions of all men and women. Then, there will be a new heaven and a new earth with harmony and peace.

Don't know much about history? Maybe now you will be motivated to dive into this world of ideas as you read about the past. This week will help you take the plunge.

WEEK 11, DAY 1

CHRISTIANITY AND HISTORY

BALONEY DETECTORS

We all know that baloney is not *real* meat. It's just animal parts that are spiced up and mashed together. It's a cheap imitation of the real thing.

In the same way, some ideas are "baloney," cheap imitations of the truth. The apostle Paul talked about detecting baloney when he said in **Colossians 2:8**,

> *Be careful that no one takes you captive through philosophy and empty deceit based on human tradition, based on the elemental forces of the world, and not based on Christ.*

Hollow ideas . . . deceptive philosophies . . . a bunch of baloney; cheap imitations of the truth.

The world is a war-zone of ideas. Hostile worldviews are competing for your allegiance. As in any war, you can either be captured, or take captives.

TAKING THOUGHTS CAPTIVE

The next time you hear someone making a claim of some sort, turn on your baloney detector. Try it out on the following idea:

> *Don't talk to me about your religion. You just accept everything on "blind faith"!*

What baloney do you detect in those lines?

WHAT DO YOU MEAN BY THAT?

By now you should have a pretty good understanding of why you believe what you believe. When someone challenges your faith in God, the first thing you should do is to ask him or her a simple question, like: "What do you mean by 'faith'?"

Usually, they will define "faith" as a "blind acceptance of something for which there is no proof."

But is that the basis of biblical faith? Give an answer based on what you have learned during your journey into a biblical worldview:

_____

_____

> *Christians believe the basis for their worldview appeared in human history in the form of Jesus Christ about two thousand years ago. While "Christ died for our sins" is orthodox Christian theology, "Christ died" is history.* (TLAC, 147)

Think about it: "Christ died" is _____. The entire Christian worldview stands or falls on events in history: specifically the life, death and resurrection of Jesus Christ. If those historical events are not true, then there is no Christianity! That's why it's so important to add the category of history to our total picture of the world.

CONSIDER THIS!
The study of history is not optional for Christians. It is primary!

HISTORY AND THE BIBLE

> *The Christian also believes that the Bible is God's revealed Word in the form of a trustworthy book grounded in history. Thus, for the Christian, history is supremely important. Either Christ is a historical figure and the Bible is a historical document that describes God's communications with humankind and records events in the life of Christ, or the Christian faith is bankrupt (1 Corinthians 15:14).* (TLAC, 147)

According to the above text, what two things would render the Christian faith bankrupt?

(1) _____

(2) _____

If our Christian faith means anything, then it must rest on the fact of Jesus' life, death and resurrection. But how do we know that Jesus died? Because the Bible is an _____ document.

Turn back to Week 3, Days 3 and 4 and review the specific reasons for the trustworthiness of the Bible. In those two lessons, seven reasons were given. List them here:

_____ _____ _____ _____

_____ _____ _____

Psalm 119:30-35

I have chosen the way of truth; I have set Your ordinances before me.
31 I cling to Your decrees; LORD, do not put me to shame.
32 I pursue the way of Your commands, for You broaden my understanding.
33 Teach me, LORD, the meaning of Your statutes, and I will always keep them.
34 Help me understand Your instruction, and I will obey it and follow it with all my heart.
35 Help me stay on the path of Your commands, for I take pleasure in it.

NO BALONEY

A biblical worldview gives a solid basis for knowing what is true and what is not. With a trustworthy Bible as the foundation, you won't be captured by "baloney" ideas.

With this information on the importance of knowing from history what we believe, how would you now respond to the idea of "blind faith"?

_____

_____

The Bible says a lot about how its truth relates to your life. Read **Psalm 119:30-35**, and turn the words of these verses into a prayer from your heart to God.

_____

_____

_____

_____

DAY 1 SUMMARY

How does history reassure you that your worldview is not based on baloney?

_____

_____

WEEK 11 KEY VERSE

Colossians 3:4 *When the Messiah, who is your life, is revealed, then you also will be revealed with Him in glory.*

WEEK 11, DAY 2

THE BIBLE AND HISTORY

ONE VERY IMPORTANT QUESTION

When considering the claims of Christianity, one question must be asked immediately: Can we trust the Bible to tell us the truth about God's actions in history? (TLAC, 147)

Think about it. You are basing your life and your whole future (eternity is a long time!) on what some book says! Maybe you had better be sure that book is a reliable source.

Yesterday, you reviewed several reasons why the Bible is true. Today, we will zero in on three areas that are important in judging the trustworthiness of the Bible from a historical perspective.

THE QUESTION OF AUTHORSHIP

Who wrote the Bible? If you take a religion course in most universities today, the professor will tell you that the book of Matthew was not written by one of Jesus' apostles, but by some unknown scribe who had not known Jesus personally. How would you respond to the professor's remarks?

_____

_____

If you were sitting in class when the professor made that remark, it would be a good time to bring out your baloney detector. The professor just made a truth-claim about the Bible. He alleged that the Bible is not to be trusted because it was written long after the events actually took place. If this were true, then, according to the professor, there would be time for myths to creep into the re-telling of the story before it was written down. But is that really how the Bible was written?

Today's scholars have little doubt that the books of the Bible were written largely by eye-witnesses. William F. Albright, a leading twentieth-century archaeologist, writes, "In my opinion, every book of the New Testament was written by a baptized Jew between the forties and the eighties of the first century (very probably sometime between about A.D. 50 and 75)." (TLAC, 148)

The fact is, the Bible was written by eyewitnesses to the events it describes. What makes that so important?

_____

2 Peter 1:16-19

For we did not follow cleverly contrived myths when we made know to you the power and coming of our Lord Jesus Christ; instead, we were eyewitnesses of His majesty. [17] For when He received honor and glory from God the Father, a voice came to Him from the Majestic Glory:

This is My beloved Son. I take delight in Him!

[18] And we heard this voice when it came from heaven while we were with Him on the holy mountain. [19] So we have the prophetic word strongly confirmed. You will do well to pay attention to it, as to a lamp shining in a dismal place, until the day dawns and the morning star arises in your hearts.

See **John 21:19-25** and **Luke 1:1-4** in the Scripture Supplement on page 205.

EYEWITNESSES IN THE NEW TESTAMENT

List the reasons that each of the following writers of the New Testament is a reliable source of information about the life, works, death, and resurrection of Jesus.

Peter: **2 Peter 1:16-19** _____

John: **John 21:19-25** _____

Luke: **Luke 1:1-4** _____

Paul: **1 Corinthians 15:3-8** _____

Galatians 1:18-19 _____

History scholars generally agree that it takes more than twenty or thirty years for legends or myths to develop. But the New Testament was written by men who were living during the time of Jesus!

WHAT ABOUT ALL THOSE COPIES?

As it turns out, archaeology has consistently confirmed that the Bible is a trustworthy historical document.

When the Bible mentions names, places and dates, archaeological discoveries confirm those names, places and dates! Can you trust a historical document like that?

HEADLINE NEWS

THE DAILY TIMES

A bit of mystery surrounds the discovery of the Dead Sea Scrolls in 1947. Some claim that the young man who found the first cave containing ancient Bible manuscripts was a simple shepherd; others suggest that he may have been involved in a smuggling operation. Regardless of his occupation, his discovery rocked the archaeological world.

One of the first Dead Sea Scrolls reproduced almost the entire book of Isaiah, in a manuscript more than 1,000 years older than what was previously thought to be the oldest manuscript. Incredibly, this ancient text was virtually identical to the modern Hebrew book of Isaiah!

This discovery, along with the subsequent discovery of fragments of almost every Old Testament book in nearby caves, reinforced the Christian assertion that the Bible is a trustworthy historical document that has not been corrupted by copyists. The Dead Sea Scrolls, and all relevant historical evidence, support the belief that the Bible provides an accurate account of actual people and events.

Read the above newspaper article, and write a headline that would catch people's attention.

_____

_____

SOMETHING TO GET EXCITED ABOUT!

It has been said that the heart cannot rejoice in what the mind rejects! Is your heart rejoicing? Are you excited about being a Christian? If not, maybe it's because your mind has been taken captive by baseless, hostile ideas concerning the historical reliability of the Bible.

Spend a few minutes considering the evidence presented in today's session. Pray that God would confirm in your mind the trustworthiness of His Book, and then allow your feelings to express real excitement over the fact that you are basing your life on the truth!

DAY 2 SUMMARY

What one historical fact about the biblical writers most supports the reliability of the Bible?

_____

DIGGING DEEPER: _For more on the historical reliability of the Bible, search any of the articles found at the Tektonitron Encyclopedia Apologetica website at www.tektonics.org/index2.html._

1 Corinthians 15:3-8

For I passed on to you as most important what I also received: that Christ died for our sins according to the Scriptures, ⁴that He was buried, that He was raised on the third day according to the Scriptures, ⁵and that He appeared to Cephas, then to the Twelve. ⁶Then He appeared to over five hundred brothers at one time, most of whom remain to the present, but some have fallen asleep. ⁷Then He appeared to James, then to all the apostles. ⁸Last of all, as to one abnormally born, He also appeared to me.

Galatians 1:18-19

Then after three years I did go up to Jerusalem to get to know Cephas, and I stayed with him fifteen days. ¹⁹But I didn't see any of the other apostles except James, the Lord's brother.

WEEK 11, DAY 3

JESUS AND HISTORY

IT SOUNDS LIKE A SQUIRREL TO ME

In Sunday school one morning a ten-year-old boy was asked by his teacher to name something that is brown, furry and eats nuts. The boy thought for a moment and said, "I know the answer must be 'Jesus,' but it sure sounds like a squirrel to me!"

It often seems like the answer to any question asked in Sunday school is "Jesus," "God," or "the Bible," and there's a reason for that. By now you realize that when it comes to a biblical worldview, the answer really is Jesus! In fact, Christian theologians agree that Christianity stands or falls on one thing. Can you name that one, specific thing that undergirds all of Christianity?

_____

THE RESURRECTION FACTOR

Jesus' resurrection is the key to Christianity and, as such, is a major issue for Christians! So major, in fact, that it sets Christianity apart from every other religion.

JESUS, A GREAT MORAL TEACHER, BUT . . .

Because of the centrality of Christ's resurrection, opponents of Christianity have tried to deny that Jesus actually rose from the dead. Walk onto most university campuses in America today, and you will hear professors of religion say something like this:

> *Jesus was a great moral teacher, but he was not God. Jesus did not come back from the dead; it was just his teachings about loving others that "came alive" in the hearts of his followers.*

Any baloney going on there? How do you respond to comments like these?

_____

_____

> *The faith of modern-day Christians should be no less secure than that of the apostles because it is grounded in historical fact. This fact forms the basis for the biblical Christian worldview and the Christian philosophy of history.* (TLAC, 151)

We have already discussed the trustworthiness of the Bible and the fact that the New Testament was written by eyewitnesses to the life of Jesus or individuals close to the actual eyewitnesses.

But who, exactly, were these people? What did they have to say about the resurrection? And why did they say it? Knowing the answer to these questions will help you respond to skeptics who reject the idea that Jesus was God.

EYEWITNESS TESTIMONY

The resurrected Christ was witnessed by more than 500 people (1 Corinthians 15:6), including Mary, Peter, and ten other apostles. These witnesses were so moved by the resurrection that they committed their lives to it and to the One whose divinity and righteousness it vindicated. . . . If the disciples did not consider the resurrection a historical event, is it really conceivable that they would be willing to die for this kind of testimony? (TLAC, 151)

Look back at 1 Corinthians 15:3-8 (on page 193). What is it that leads you to the conclusion that Jesus was physically raised from the dead?

_____

List the individuals or groups of people who saw the resurrected Jesus:

(1) _____

(2 _____

(3) _____

(4 _____

(5) _____

(6 _____

Think about Jesus' disciples; what kind of men and women were they (see **John 20:19,25**)?

_____

_____

_____

John 20:19,25

20:19   In the evening of that first day of the week, the disciples were gathered together with the doors locked because of their fear of the Jews. Then Jesus came, stood among them, and said to them, "Peace to you!"

20:25   So the other disciples kept telling him, "We have seen the Lord!"

But he said to them, "If I don't see the mark of the nails in His hands, put my finger into the mark of the nails, and put my hand into His side, I will never believe."

Acts 4:18-21

So they called for them and ordered them not to preach or teach at all in the name of Jesus. ¹⁹But Peter and John answered them, "Whether it's right in the sight of God for us to listen to you rather than to God, you decide; ²⁰for we are unable to stop speaking about what we have seen and heard." ²¹After threatening them further, they released them. They found no way to punish them, because the people were all giving glory to God over what had been done. . . .

Acts 5:17-21

Then the high priest took action. He and all his colleagues, those who belonged to the party of the Sadducees, were filled with jealousy. ¹⁸So they arrested the apostles and put them in the city jail. ¹⁹But an angel of the Lord opened the doors of the jail during the night, brought them out, and said, ²⁰"Go and stand in the temple complex, and tell the people all about this life." ²¹In obedience to this, they entered the temple complex at daybreak and began to teach.

After the resurrection, how did they change? (See **Acts 4:18-21** and **5:17-21**.)

_____

_____

What did they claim made the difference in their attitudes and actions? (Look at **Acts 4:8-13** in the Scripture Supplement on page 205 .)

_____

_____

Based on the historical fact of the resurrection of Jesus, how sure are you about your faith in Christ? Mark an "X" to represent where you are on the following "Assurance" scale:

0%   50%   100%

|___|___|___|___|___|___|___|___|___|___|

APPLYING *HISTORY* TO *YOUR* STORY

Are you confident in your faith? Is it based on the facts of history? Is there any reason for not believing the testimony of the disciples?

 PRAY ABOUT IT!

Take a few minutes in prayer to thank God for making Jesus' resurrection a solid historical fact, a fact so secure that you can trust your life to it.

DAY 3 SUMMARY

What is it about the historical record of Jesus that shows us that He was not just "a great moral teacher"?

_____

_____

WEEK 11 KEY VERSE:

Colossians 3:4 *When the _____, who is your life, is revealed, then you also will be revealed with Him in glory.*

WEEK 11, DAY 4

HISTORY AND YOU

HISTORY WITH A PURPOSE

Have you ever asked the question, "What is my purpose in life?" That question, when asked on a personal level, actually implies a more far-reaching question: Is there any purpose to life in general? In other words, does God have a plan and purpose for history?

A biblical worldview informs us that God does, in fact, have a plan. This plan for humanity is played out through the events that have happened in the past, through what is taking place today, and even includes what will happen in the future. His wonderful plan also involves you!

> *This belief about God's actions in history has vast ramifications for mankind. If the Christian philosophy of history is correct, then not only is the overall story of mankind invested with meaning, but every moment that man lives is charged with purpose.*
> (TLAC, 153)

"Every moment that man lives is charged with _____." Do you believe that? Is your life charged with purpose?

Let's get a biblical perspective on that last question about purpose in life. To do that, we have to step back and get a "Big Picture" view of God's purpose for His creation. From that vantage point, we can focus on His purpose for your life.

THE BIG PICTURE

First, read from **Acts 17:**

26   From one man He has made every nation of men to live all over the earth and has determined their appointed times and the boundaries of where they live,

27   so that they might seek God, and perhaps they might reach out and find Him, though He is not far from each one of us.

28   For in Him we live and move and exist, . . .

Who is the "one man" Paul refers to in verse 26?

_____

What is the point Paul draws from the fact that Adam is the first man?

_____

Verse 27 gives a purpose statement when it says God did this "so that. . . ." Why did God determine the times set for each man?

_____

_____

What is the conclusion found in verse 28?

_____

_____

Fill in the blanks to amplify verse 28:

      for in Him (God)

        we (Paul, you and everyone else)

          live (_____)

            and move (_____)

            and exist (_____)

MORE MEANING FOR YOUR LIFE!

> *From the Christian perspective, history is a beautiful unfolding of God's ultimate plan for mankind. Does this mean, however, that only the future holds any value for the Christian? Does the Christian worldview destroy the role of the present in history? The answer is a resounding "no." In the Christian view, God is active throughout history. Therefore, this perspective creates more meaning for every moment of time. . . .* (TLAC, 152)

History is the progression of time, and you are currently living it. God is active right now, and the above quote applies to you. Because of His plan and purpose there is "more _____ for every moment of time" in your life.

Do you realize that God has already revealed His purpose and plan for you? It involves all the principles and ideas found in the Bible. This study of a biblical Christian worldview has introduced you to many of the plans God has in each area of life. For example, in **theology,** you learned that God is relational. Given that, what is God's plan for you regarding your relationship to Him? In simple language: God's plan is for you to enter into a relationship with Him by accepting Jesus' payment for your sin problem.

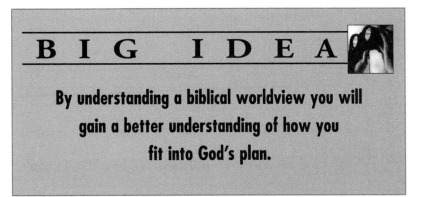

BIG IDEA

By understanding a biblical worldview you will
gain a better understanding of how you
fit into God's plan.

In **philosophy**, you realized that you could know what is true in the world by studying God's general revelation (His world) and His special revelation (His Word). In light of this, what should be one of your goals in life?

_____

The study on **biology** demonstrated that you are a created being. This gives significance to your life because:

_____

_____

_____

Biblical **ethics** revealed that God has established certain moral guidelines for living. How does that intersect your life?

_____

_____

_____

Mankind is created in God's image, yet is fallen into sin, according to Christian **psychology**. This idea relates to you in what two ways?

1) _____

2) _____

The family is a significant part of God's plan according to biblical **sociology**. What does that imply about God's work in your life?

- ☐ Marriage can be defined any way I want it to be.
- ☐ Living together without being officially married is okay as long as we love each other.
- ☐ Being married and raising children are probably a part of God's plan for me, so I need to prepare myself for being a partner and a parent.

James 1:5

Now if any of you lacks wisdom, he should ask God, who gives to all generously and without criticizing, and it will be given to him.

What is the main point of biblical **law**, and how does that apply to you?

Main point:

_____

Application:

_____

God has a plan for **politics**. So, how should you relate to our system of government?

_____

In the area of **economics**, God's will for your life revolves around how you make and spend money and use other resources. How is this significant to you?

_____

_____

If God has revealed Himself and His ways throughout **history**, what does that imply about how you apply yourself to understand the past?

_____

DAY 4 SUMMARY

Why should you believe that God has a specific plan for your life?

_____

_____

 PERSONAL APPLICATION

Spend some time praying for His wisdom to understand how you fit into His plan (See **James 1:5**).

WEEK 11, DAY 5

THE DIRECTION OF HISTORY

INVASION OF THE . . .

Alien invasions from outer space have been a popular theme of Hollywood filmmakers over the years. If someone asked you, you could probably name your favorite alien movie.

But there is another type of invasion that is not science fiction. In place of a one-time, war-like attack on mankind, this invasion has had a lasting, positive effect on the human race. Not only that, there is a second invasion scheduled to take place in the future. This invasion will have an impact of "world-changing" proportions. Can you name each of these two invasions?

Past invasion: _____

Future invasion: _____

The two invasions refer to a time when the supernatural invaded the natural world. It has happened once already when God became a Man and walked this planet. The birth of Jesus Christ marked the first invasion. The second divine invasion will take place when Jesus comes again to establish His visible kingdom on planet Earth.

DIRECTION, WHAT DIRECTION?

> *This Christian belief about the direction of history is known as a linear conception of history. That is, Christians believe that human history had a specific beginning (creation) and is being directed by God toward a specific end (judgment), and that historic events follow a nonrepetitive course toward that end.* (TLAC, 154)

Write in your own words what the "linear" concept of history implies?

_____

_____

Although God is in control of the direction of history and will bring it to an end, the Bible also is clear that you have a part in the process. You can make choices that affect your life and your future.

WHAT THE FUTURE HOLDS

Some people consult the Psychic Hotline to try to peer into the future. But Christians have something better. God has told us what the future has in store.

2 Peter 3:13-14

But based on His promise, we wait for new heavens and a new earth, where righteousness will dwell.
¹⁴ Therefore, dear friends, while you wait for these things, make every effort to be found in peace without spot or blemish before Him.

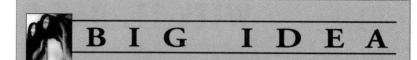

BIG IDEA

The linear concept of history means that history is going in a straight line, headed in a certain direction.

For the Christian, history is moving toward a specific climax: the Day of Judgment (Acts 17:31; Romans 2:11-16). At this point, Christ's victory over sin will become apparent to everyone, and Christians from all of history will be allowed to share in His triumph. (TLAC, 153)

How will we share in His triumph? Read the exciting details concerning Christ's victory in **1 Corinthians 15:51-57** (see the Scripture Supplement on page 205). Write any thoughts or questions you have from reading these verses:

_____

_____

_____

A NEW HOME. . . RIGHT HERE ON PLANET EARTH

There is something else that God has in store for us in the future. Read **2 Peter 3:13-14** to find out what it is.

History reaches its climax when God judges sin and establishes a new _____ and new _____.

The book of Revelation describes this as our new home where we will dwell eternally with Him in peace and splendor (**Revelation 21** and **22**). What a beautiful ending to the story of history! It began at creation and ends with a re-creation of a place for all believers to live.

LIVING BETWEEN THE TWO INVASIONS

While the new earth will be a wonderful place, there is still a lot of living to do in the here and now. On the timeline of history, we are living between the two invasions of Jesus' first and second comings. What should we be doing during this "in-between" time? Our biblical worldview holds the answer.

Read **Matthew 13:24-30** (see the Scriptural Supplement on page 206), and write what you find takes place during this "in-between" time?

_____

_____

_____

_____

GROWING WEEDS IN GOD'S GARDEN

In **Matthew 13:36-43** (see the Scriptural Supplement on page 206), Jesus explains that two things will be growing at the same time. First, His church will grow as Christians go throughout world to share the good news of God's love and forgiveness. This represents the _____ growing in the field.

But what about the weeds? They represent non-Christians who also will increase during this age. However, there will be a time in the future when God judges the world and removes those who do evil.

Since this "in-between" time will see the growth of evil in the world, should we just resign ourselves to this increasing evil and not try to do anything about it? Or is there a better course of action for Christians to take?

WHAT TO DO?

Again, God has given us directions on what we should do during the "in-between" time. Read **Titus 2:11-14.** What is our responsibility before the end will come?

_____

Titus 2:11-14

For the grace of God has appeared, with salvation for all people, [12]instructing us to deny godlessness and worldly lusts and to live in a sensible, righteous, and godly way in the present age, [13]while we wait for the blessed hope and the appearing of the glory of our great God and Savior, Jesus Christ. [14]He gave Himself for us to redeem us from all lawlessness and to cleanse for Himself a special people, eager to do good works.

IT MAKES A DIFFERENCE IN YOUR LIFE

> *Christian history centers on the reliability of the Bible. . . . If this historical perspective is correct, then the Christian worldview is proved to be true, and it follows that knowing, accepting, and following Jesus Christ as Savior and Lord is the most important thing anyone can do. Wise men still seek Him, and for good reason. He gives meaning to history, and to life.* (TLAC, 155)

What is the most important thing a person can do?

_____

_____

Why is knowing and following Jesus Christ as Savior and Lord so crucial?

_____

_____

In what ways do you plan to follow Jesus as Lord?

_____

_____

DAY 5 SUMMARY

What is the biblical understanding of the direction of history?

_____

_____

WEEK 11 KEY VERSE

Colossians 3:4 *When the Messiah, who is your life, is revealed, then you also will be revealed with Him in* _____.

WEEK 11 SUMMARY

Christianity is a historical religion. It is the story of God's dealing with humanity from the creation of time to the climax of His judgment and re-creation of a new heaven and new earth. The Bible is a reliable source about historical people, places and events. The most significant event it records is the resurrection of Jesus Christ. Because of Jesus' death and resurrection, we can have assurance of

God's love and acceptance by placing our trust in Him as our substitute for sin. That assurance should make a difference in how we live each day of our lives.

SCRIPTURE SUPPLEMENT

Luke 1:1-4 *Since many have undertaken to compile a narrative about the events that have been fulfilled among us, [2]just as the original eyewitnesses and servants of the word handed them down to us, [3]it also seemed good to me, having carefully investigated everything from the very first, to write to you in orderly sequence, most honorable Theophilus, [4]so that you may know the certainty of the things about which you have been instructed.*

Acts 4:8-13 *Then Peter was filled with the Holy Spirit and said to them, "Rulers of the people and elders: [9]If we are being examined today about a good deed done to a disabled man—by what means he was healed—[10]let it be known to all of you and to all the people of Israel, that by the name of Jesus Christ the Nazarene—whom you crucified and whom God raised from the dead—by Him this man is standing here before you healthy. [11]This Jesus is*

> *The stone despised by you builders,*
>
> *who has become the cornerstone.*

[12]There is salvation in no one else, for there is no other name under heaven given to people by which we must be saved."

[13]Observing the boldness of Peter and John and realizing them to be uneducated and untrained men, they were amazed and knew that they had been with Jesus.

1 Corinthians 15:51-57 *Listen! I am telling you a mystery:*

> *We will not all fall asleep, but we will all be changed,*

[52]in a moment, in the twinkling of an eye, at the last trumpet. For the dead will be raised incorruptible, and we will be changed.

[53]Because this corruptible must be clothed with incorruptibility, and this mortal must be clothed with immortality.

[54]Now when this corruptible is clothed with incorruptibility, and this mortal is clothed with immortality, then the saying that is written will take place; Death has been swallowed up in victory.

[55]O Death, where is your victory? O Death, where is your sting?

[56]Now the sting of death is sin, and the power of sin is the law.

[57]But thanks be to God, who gives us the victory through our Lord Jesus Christ!

Matthew 13:24-30 *He presented another parable to them: "The kingdom of heaven may be compared to a man who sowed good seed in his field. 25 But while people were sleeping, his enemy came, sowed weeds among the wheat, and left. 26 When the plants sprouted and produced grain, then the weeds also appeared. 27 The landowner's slaves came to him and said, 'Master, didn't you sow good seed in your field? Then where did the weeds come from?'*

28 "An enemy did this!' he told them.

"So, do you want us to go and gather them up?' the slaves asked him.

29 "No,' he said. 'When you gather up the weeds, you might also uproot the wheat with them. 30 Let both grow together until the harvest. At harvest time I'll tell the reapers, "Gather the weeds first and tie them in bundles to burn them, but store the wheat in my barn."'"

Matthew 13:36-43 *Then He dismissed the crowds and went into the house. And His disciples approached Him and said, "Explain the parable of the weeds in the field to us."*

37 He replied: "The One who sows the good seed is the Son of Man; 38 the field is the world; and the good seed—these are the sons of the kingdom. The weeds are the sons of the evil one, and 39 the enemy who sowed them is the Devil. The harvest is the end of the age, and the harvesters are angels. 40 Therefore just as the weeds are gathered and burned in the fire, so it will be at the end of the age. 41 The Son of Man will send out His angels, and they will gather from His kingdom everything that causes sin and those guilty of lawlessness. 42 They will throw them into the blazing furnace where there will be weeping and gnashing of teeth. 43 Then the righteous will shine like the sun in their Father's kingdom. Anyone who has ears should listen!"

John 21:19-25 *He [Jesus] said this to signify by what kind of death he [Peter] would glorify God. After saying this, He told him, "Follow Me!" 20 So Peter tuned around and saw the disciple Jesus loved following them. That disciple was the one who had leaned back against Jesus at the supper and asked, "Lord, who is the one that's going to betray You?" 21 When Peter saw him, he said to Jesus, "Lord—what about him?" 22 "If I want him to remain until I come," Jesus answered, "what is that to you? As for you, follow Me." 23 So this report spread to the brothers that this disciple would not die. Yet Jesus did not tell him that he would not die, but "If I want him to remain until I come, what is that to you?" 24 This is the disciple who testifies to these things and who wrote them down. We know that his testimony is true. 25 And there are also many other things that Jesus did, which, if they were written one by one, I suppose not even the world itself could contain the books that would be written.*

A FINAL CHALLENGE

BIBLICAL CHRISTIANITY IN RETREAT

This course of study has taken you through a biblical Christian worldview. But as you look around, you'll notice that our society is moving away from Christian principles in every area that we have studied.

> *The Christian worldview is in retreat in nearly every arena of American life—including our universities, media, arts, music, law, business, medicine, psychology, sociology, public schools, and government. "The humanistic system of values has now become the predominant way of thinking in most of the power centers of society," claim James C. Dobson and Gary L. Bauer. According to Dobson and Bauer, the Christian worldview has only two power centers remaining in America—the church and the family—and both of them are under tremendous pressure to surrender.* (TLAC, 166-7)

What are the signs of our time that indicate Christianity is in retreat in some of the areas listed above?

_____

_____

According to James Dobson and Gary Bauer, what is the predominant worldview in our country today?

_____

Humanism is a religious system of thought that starts with man instead of God. It is a total worldview that comes in three prominent forms in Western civilization: Secular Humanism, Marxism-Leninism, and Cosmic Humanism (New Age Pantheism and Neo-Paganism).

These humanist philosophies seek to tear down the biblical foundations that have supported our nation for over 300 years and Western civilization for over 2,000 years. Many social commentators point out that the breakdown of society is a result of the influence of these non-Christian worldviews and the retreat of the church from society! As you consider all the problems our country faces, do you want to be a part of the problem, or a part of the solution?

WHAT'S A BODY TO DO?

There are some things that you can do to have a positive impact on our culture and our world.

> *What are we to do? Go on the offensive! Light a candle (Matthew 5:14). Pray (2 Chronicles 7:14; Colossians 1:9-14). Study (2 Timothy 2:15). Understand the times (1 Chronicles 12:32). Rebuild the foundations (Psalm 11:3). Spread the word with courage and conviction (Hebrews 11; 1 Peter 3:15-16). Truth is our greatest weapon.* (TLAC, 167)

So don't just sit there, do something! For each of the above suggestions, prayerfully add a specific thing you can do to make it a reality in your life:

(1) Light a candle (What can you do in a positive way to make a difference in your local school or community?):

_____

(2) _____: For what, specifically? _____

_____

(3) _____: You can start by going to the Summit Ministries website (www.summit.org) for a suggested reading list.

(4) _____ the times (What can you do to be better informed about the ideas and trends in our culture): _____

(5) Rebuild the _____ (Before you can rebuild the foundations, you must understand the ideas that our society is founded upon. How can you do that? When will you do it?):

_____

_____

(6) _____ the word (Make a list of people close to you who need to hear the word.)

_____   _____

_____   _____

MAKING IT HAPPEN

Why not share this list with some friends who will pray with you? Enlist them as a support team to help you accomplish your action points! Write their names here:

_____   _____

 ## A CLOSING PRAYER

As a closing prayer for this study of a biblical Christian worldview, meditate on **1 Peter 3:15**, and ask God to bring to mind what you need to do to confront our world with the truth of God's Word:

> *But set apart the Messiah as Lord in your hearts,*
> *and always be ready to give a defense to anyone*
> *who asks you a reason for the hope that is in you.*

NOTES

NOTES

NOTES

NOTES

NOTES

NOTES

NOTES

NOTES